# A Painful Season
## &
# A Stubborn Hope

# A Painful Season
## &
# A Stubborn Hope

*The Odyssey of an Eritrean Mother*

by
Abeba Tesfagiorgis

**THE RED SEA PRESS, INC.**
*Publishers and Distributors of Third World Books*
11 Princess Road, Suite D
Lawrenceville, New Jersey 08648

**The Red Sea Press, Inc.**
11 Princess Road, Suite D
Lawrenceville, NJ 08648

Copyright © Abeba Tesfagiorgis, 1992
First Printing, 1992
Second Printing, April 1995

Disclaimer: The author has chosen to use fictitious names for some of those mentioned in the book. In particular the names of her cell mates, some of the people she met in Port Sudan, and the names of some of the fighters in Eritrea are fictitious.

Cover & Book Design by Jonathan Gullery
This book is composed in Palatino

Library of Congress Cataloging in Publication Data

Abeba Tesfagiorgis.
 A painful season & a stubborn hope : the odyssey of an Eritrean woman in prison / by Abeba Tesfagiorgis.
  p. cm
 ISBN 0-932415-83-0 (cloth) : $39.95 — ISBN 0-932415-84-9 (pbk.)
 : $12.95
  1. Abeba Tesfagiorgis. 2. Political prisioners—Ethiopia—Eritrea
 —Biography. 3. Women political prisoners—Ethiopia—Eritrea
 —Biography 4. Eritrea (Ethiopia)--History--Revolution. 1962-1991.
 I. Title. II. Title: Painful season and a stubborn hope.
 HV9844.5.A114    1992
 365'.45'092--dc20
 [B]                                              92-14196
                                                     CIP

*for my daughters*
*Ruth, Tamar, Muzit, and Senait*
*and my late mother*

# Acknowledgments

Many people encouraged and helped me in many ways during the course of writing this account of a particular, turbulent period in my life.

Dr. Araia Tseggai, Pat Clendenin, Brendan Griffin, Dr. Haile Mezghebe, Karen Hauser, Evelyn Richardson, John Edwin Smith, Tsehai Habtemariam, Tsion Tesfai, Tamara Yohannes, Wubet Tesfamichael, read all or parts of the manuscript and offered many suggestions. For their various comments, and for their support I am extremely grateful.

I owe a special debt of gratitude to Thomas Keneally, author of the inspiring novel, *To Asmara,* which deals with the Eritrean struggle, for taking the time to read my first draft and for his generosity of spirit.

I would like to thank my husband, Mesfun Hailu, for helping me with some of the details of the book and for his his moral support.

I am most grateful to my sister-in-law, Michealin Baatai, for spending many long hours reviewing the manuscript and for serving as my best critic.

When I gave my manuscript to my long-time friend, Mehret Ghebreyesus, for review, her face beamed and with tears in her eyes said: "So we Eritreans have now a recorded story of some of our personal pains in the struggle." I am grateful for her support and valuable comments on the manuscript.

My heartfelt thanks go to my brother Paulos Tesfagiorghis who encouraged me to come from Dallas to his temporary home in Montreal and gave me invaluable moral support during the editing and re-writing of the manuscript. He also carefully reviewed the final drafts and helped me to develop and articulate some of the ideas expressed herein. Paulos took it upon himself to make sure that I saw this record of my experiences through to completion. His love and kindness know no bounds.

I am indebted to my editor, Jane Broderick, who took a great deal of interest in my story as well as in the history and people of Eritrea, and whose endless hours poring over the several drafts of the manuscript went well beyond the call of duty.

# Foreword

This remarkable book is the story, told in her own words, of a brave woman who held out strongly, and with full success, against vicious persecution and violence. Abeba Tesfagiorgis is an Eritrean from Asmara in East Africa. She comes from a people who have had to confront and overcome long years of colonial invasion and occupation of their country. But although this is in many ways a painful story, it is not a sad story. Like tens of thousands of her fellow-countrywomen and men, Abeba accepted the duty and need to resist oppression and injustice; and because of their courage and self-sacrifice the story that Abeba tells, of her companions as of herself, is as inspiring in its message of hope and sanity as it is modest and self-disregarding in the way she tells it for us.

The message comes to us because the Eritreans won free from colonial fetters at the end of the 1980s, and have since begun to shape a life of their own for the first time in many decades. They were able to win this victory over evil for many reasons of stubborn and intelligent persistence, but above all because they were able to forge among themselves a unity of companionship in struggle that proved invincible. We learn to understand this through Abeba's experiences. A socially privileged person, normally with a good and safe job in Asmara, Eritrea's capital city, and raised in the respect of conventional and everyday social values, Abeba Tesfagiorgis nonetheless chose the harsh and perilous road of revolt. In following this road through every squalor of intimidation, she found her way to the heart of the people.

I think this is a story for everyone to whom freedom and justice are not negotiable, no matter what dangers and difficulties they may impose upon people who struggle for them. Abeba Tesfagiorgis asked me to write some words to introduce her book. I do it with a feeling of being greatly honored. Every reader, having read this book, will share that feeling with me.

Basil Davidson

# One

On the twenty-ninth of September 1975, at ten o'clock in the morning, I had a telephone call from a good friend, Padre Angelico Woldezion, a Catholic priest at the main cathedral, which was just a block away from the Ethiopian Airlines office in Asmara, where I worked.

When Padre Angelico said "*Selam*"—Hello! I detected a relaxed air that I had not sensed in him for months. He had been busy not only with masses and the usual heavy schedule of weddings, baptisms, and burials, but also with helping needy mothers and children through churches and various organizations in Asmara and many other parts of Eritrea.

"You won't believe my news," he said excitedly.

"What is it?" I asked. There was a pause. "If you need me," I added, "I can come over right away."

"No," Padre Angelico replied, "I'll be there shortly."

Perhaps, I thought, there has been a stunning victory by our freedom fighters — the *tegadelti*. He could have received the good news secretly from his friends in Rome.

My speculations went far and wide during the short wait for Padre Angelico's visit. Then the swinging door to the airline office opened and I was indeed surprised by the sight, for accompanying Padre Angelico was the lively Padre Michael — or Padre Agatangelo, as he is usually called — from Agordat.

I embraced Padre Michael and kissed the hands of both priests, as is the custom.

"It must be close to a year since we saw each other in Agordat, Padre. What brings you here?" I asked. I gestured for them to sit.

As he settled into his chair and began to speak, I noticed that behind Padre Micael's broad smile was a very tired face indeed.

"It is exactly ten months and a week, in fact, since I saw you in Agordat at the meeting in our church," he said. "You've lost weight, Abeba. Well, that's to be expected, I suppose. How are Mesfun and the children?"

"Abeba knows that I always give you news of her and her family when I write," said Padre Angelico to his friend.

"But you never mentioned that she has become so thin."

"Do I have to give every little detail?" was Padre Angelico's reply, and we all laughed.

Padre Micael grew very serious all of a sudden: "Do you remember the teacher who sat next to you at our meeting?"

"Yes. And I heard he was thrown into prison. Is he still there?"

"No... well..." Padre Micael cast his eyes downward.

"You mean... he's gone... killed?"

"Yes."

I was saddened and angered at the same time by this news. Before I had a chance to say anything, though, or to ask for more information, I was interrupted by a telephone call and three customers who came to see the district manager. Normally, I would have taken the priests to the privacy of the conference room, or to the café Lateria Moderna downstairs, but now I was too busy.

I directed the three customers to the manager's office and then called my husband. Mesfun was pleased that Padre Micael was in town, and suggested we have both men over for lunch the next day. Padre Micael accepted readily, while Padre Angelico agreed only at my insistence.

"Then it's one o'clock tomorrow — I can't wait," I said, showing them out. As the two priests descended the stairs, my eye caught the large silver crosses dangling from the ropes around their waists. How long are we going to bear our heavy crosses, Lord? I asked silently. Now the teacher who was so full of life had joined the countless others who ask for nothing but freedom.

There was no time to dwell on our burdens however. I went about my office work, first telephoning home to tell Shashu, our maid, that we would be having two guests over for lunch the following day.

I felt a great sense of elation when I woke up early that last day of September and went to the garden to cut carnations for the dining-room table and for the living room. I had been neglecting the garden for some time, but the gardener had been weeding it regularly and it was in fairly good shape. For some reason I gave extra hugs to my children as they went off to school on that fateful day. They all looked especially beautiful in their green and white, yellow and blue uniforms.

Because we had paid help and a large home with every convenience, it was always a pleasure to entertain guests, even in the uncertain and grim atmosphere of our national life. Our friendships had become ever more invaluable at that particular time in our nation's history, when lives were being snatched away and one knew not what the next day would bring — or the next hour, for that matter.

Padre Angelico had his own car, so the two priests were right on time. Mesfun rushed out to the gate to embrace Padre Micael. I'm sure Padre Micael had many heartbreaking stories to tell, (and we did as well) but he must have decided not to dwell on the upsetting subject of the conflict after seeing my reaction to the news of the teacher in Agordat. In any case, we all tacitly agreed to make the best of our ninety minutes together.

For the first time in nine months, we ate in the dining room, — the china, silverware, and crystal adding a touch of elegance. We feasted on lasagna with roasted chicken and green salad, although only bananas and oranges were available for dessert. Guests usually looked forward to imported cheese and Swiss chocolate at our home, but Mesfun and I had had to put such luxuries out of our minds for the time being.

We savoured the food and the company; it was just like the good old days. We were in the habit of inviting Padre Angelico often, but he usually declined, saying he would feel guilty sitting down to enjoy a four-course meal. Today, happily, he relaxed and laughed at Padre Micael's jokes about the Dergue — the Marxist military regime that had taken power in Ethiopia in 1974, after ousting Emperor Haile Selassie. Padre Angelico closed our joyful meal with a short prayer: "May God be with our children — our fighters — and may the suffering come to an end."

"We know very well that ultimate victory will be ours. The Dergue can kill only our flesh, not our souls," said Padre Micael. "Anyway, let's be off before they hear about our meal. If they suspect it, they'll split open our bellies to see how much good food we have eaten," he joked.

At half past two, the guests left and my husband and I returned to our offices. I was working on the 1976 district budget that day, and I was using the conference room so that I could spread out all my papers.

I worked all afternoon, losing myself in the dizzying sea of numbers. Then, at half past four, two young men in khaki suits burst into the conference room without knocking. I was totally absorbed in my work, head bent over columns of figures, pencil in hand.

"Are you Woizero Abeba Tesfagiorgis?" asked one of the intruders insolently, having some difficulty keeping the decorum required by addressing me as "Mrs."

I wanted to say: It is none of your business who I am. Just get out of here. But my very nature, coupled with my many years of working in a variety of service organisations, militated against such an indignant response. Instead, I answered:

"Yes, I am. What can I do for you?"

"Sorry to interrupt, but we have to talk to you urgently."

"I'm working on the budget and don't have a moment to spare, so why don't you go ahead and make it quick."

"It won't take a minute. Just follow us downstairs," said the one wearing a white shirt.

Follow us. An order! Oh, my Lord. Could it be them? I wondered. Fear shot through my body like a bolt of lightning. The other man, who was in a blue shirt, gave me a look that was clearly meant to intimidate. But I looked into his eyes and saw that he was very nervous himself.

"This isn't my office... let me get my sweater," I suggested. The telephone operator was in my office at that moment, and I smiled bravely as she handed me the sweater. She did not return the smile, however; in fact, she had an expression of utter horror on her face. As the two were escorting me from my office, a ticket agent saw us and the color drained from his face. Not knowing what to do, he turned and went into the men's room. The reactions of my two colleagues confirmed to me the identity of my abductors: They were members of the infamous *afagn*, the secret police — the hated and feared SS of Eritrea.

A white Volkswagen beetle was parked outside the ticket office. The man in the white shirt pulled a revolver from his jacket and pointed it at me.

"Quick. Get in. You have wasted enough time."

There was a man at the wheel and another in the passenger seat. My abductor in the blue shirt got in at my other side. He picked up an automatic rifle from the floor of the car and put it on his lap. I found myself sandwiched between two armed men. They shut the windows and the driver started up immediately. There was an awesome silence.

Not knowing what to say or do, I said, "Gentlemen, who are you and what am I doing here?"

The man in the passenger seat turned around to face me. "Woman, you know who we are and you know what crimes you have committed."

Then they did something very odd. They drove me very slowly around the city.

Asmara, the capital of Eritrea, was built by the Italians in 1889. It is a lovely city, many say one of the most beautiful in Africa. Situated seven thousand feet above sea level, and surrounded by hills, it enjoys clear skies and ideal temperatures — seventy-five to eighty-five degrees year-round, getting just a little chilly in the evenings and early mornings during the months of December through February. The palm trees lining the wide avenues, the three and four-story buildings, the outdoor cafés famous for their cappuccino remind visitors of some parts of Italy.

The airline for which I worked was located in the heart of the city, on what was then called Haile Selassie Avenue, and my abductors drove the length of it. I noticed that the man next to the driver was marveling at the displays of imported and local goods in the shop windows, from radios and television sets to furs, woollen sweaters, fine leather coats and shoes; from handmade silver and gold jewelery, to beautiful olivewood household articles.

We proceeded to Queen Elizabeth Avenue, past Haile Selassie Secondary School, past villas with gardens overflowing with bougainvillaea and jacaranda. Then we drove toward the main market close to the mosque, avoiding the residential areas in the northern part of the city — Edaga Arbi, Aba Shawul, Geza Kenisha.

On weekends and holidays, my husband and I would sometimes take the children for car rides into the countryside — to towns like Mendefera, Ghinda, and Keren. On the way to Ghinda, past Bet Gherghis, Arberoubu, and Nefasit on the outskirts of Asmara, the mountains reach so high into the clouds they seem to be capped with snow. The white haze drifting between the mountains, the winding roads, the valleys, the railway tunnels — all are absolutely breathtaking. The road to Keren is marvelous as well. We would often drive the five miles from Asmara to the dam, which had exquisite gardens, past Adi Abeito and the fields of wheat and barley. Eritrea was wonderful and I could never get enough of it.

Now here I was, traveling part of the same route with armed strangers, destination unknown. Were they giving me an opportunity to say goodbye to my beloved Asmara, the city where I had lived my entire life, where I was born and educated, where I was raising my children? Or were they merely trying to intimidate me?

After an hour of driving around, we headed to the *ghebi* — the palace — where the prison was located. The huge iron gate was opened and two heavily-armed sentries kept watch as we drove through. We parked just inside the gate, and the two men in front got out immediately. They bent their seats forward and the two in the back slipped out as well. "Get out," ordered the man at my right. The driver and his partner, who had a particularly sadistic way about him, got back in and drove off as soon as I had climbed out of the car, perhaps to pick up another victim.

The armed men led me up a flight of stairs and into a small room where a man entered my name and the date into a register and then demanded that I hand over my gold earrings and my watch. The room was cold and lifeless. There was only a small table, one metal chair, and a metal cupboard where prisoners' valuables were kept.

"Thank you," said my abductors to the registrar, and, with a sarcastic smile in my direction, they vanished.

Two guards appeared immediately and led me down a long corridor, one guard walking ahead of me, the other behind. As I moved through the corridor, I saw grey iron doors to my right and left and I heard hushed voices.

"Stop," said the first guard suddenly, his harsh order exploding in my ears. He surveyed me from head to toe, opened a door, and pushed me into a small cell that was already crowded with five women. He slammed the door shut with a deafening clang and noisily locked it with a finality that was terrifying.

I was consumed with anger. I felt violated.

# Two

The thirty-first of January 1975. A whole month of the fresh year had gone by remarkably quickly, and a new month would be beginning in just a matter of hours.

Office workers were home by half past six that evening, and Mesfun and I were no exception. Our house in the Geza Banda section of Asmara had been constructed in the 1930s by a well-known Italian engineer for his personal use. The two-story villa was built into the slope of a small cliff. It had five rooms when my husband and I bought it in the late 1960s, but we remodeled it completely to our taste; it was now a large home with eight rooms and three bathrooms.

The upper and lower rooms were terraced along the hill, with an outside stairway linking the two levels. Well-trimmed creepers completely covered the high stone wall at the back. Bougainvillaea embraced the low brick wall at the front. Daisies, carnations, lilies, and gladioli beautifully set off the cream-colored villa with its contrasting green gates.

There were two doors upstairs. One opened into the living room with its small anteroom and an adjacent office/library; the dining room was next to the living room. The other door opened into the kitchen, which then led to the family room and the master bedroom.

A table and six chairs occupied the center of the kitchen, and the table was always graced with a vase of flowers. Two windows taking up most of an entire wall welcomed the morning sun. In the family room were photographs of our wedding and of the children. On the wall hung a large painting of two horses grazing near a barn, one looking off into the distance and the other munching away at the grass, and this painting was always a reminder to me of the tranquil days of my childhood. It was in these two rooms, the kitchen and the family room, that we spent the greater part of our time together as a family.

The formal dining room with its big mahogany table; the spacious living room with its two sofa sets and large windows all done in lace curtains — we used mostly when we had guests, which was frequently. Downstairs were the children's bedrooms and the storage area. A separate small building in the compound served as the maids' quarters.

I would not say our house was a mansion; but my husband and I had spent considerable time and effort making it comfortable and attractive. Our friends from the West and elsewhere loved the setting of the villa and would comment on its unique decor.

As soon as she heard the sound of our car that evening, Natzenet, the housekeeper, opened the garage door. Three of our children — Tamar, Muzit, and Senait — welcomed us home with their usual smothering of hugs and kisses.

As we went in through the kitchen door, Tamar, our fourteen-year-old daughter, took my handbag, while Muzit, who was then eight, ran to the bedroom and got my slippers. Knowing that we were not going out that evening, I immediately changed into comfortable clothes, put on my slippers, kissed Tamar and Muzit for helping me, and the four of us sat, Senait taking center stage on my lap. Mesfun went directly to the library.

"How was school today? And where's Ruth?" I asked. Senait had already started playing with my gold necklace, so I took it off and put it around her neck. She jumped up and went to the mirror in our bedroom to see how she looked.

"Can I try on one of your necklaces too, Mommy? Please?" asked Muzit, after seeing Senait's triumph.

Tamar didn't wait for my answer. "Listen, Muzei, don't play around with Mommy's necklaces," she ordered. "I'll get that one back from Senu too," she added, using the girls' nicknames as she usually did. I appreciated the responsible tone Tamar was taking with her little sisters. "I'll let you wear it some other time," I told Muzit reluctantly. "Listen to your sister now." Muzit was clearly unhappy and slipped out to be consoled by her father.

Neither Tamar nor Muzit had replied when I asked them about Ruth, my eldest. Just as I was about to ask again, she came running up the stairs, making sure her bookmark was in place before she hugged me. Ruth was a voracious reader. "I didn't realize it was so late." she said. "Well, I'd better stop reading and finish my homework. Where's Papa?" And off she went to find her father, not waiting for my reply.

Tamar checked with our maids to see if dinner was ready. Natzenet, the older, was the housekeeper, while the younger Shashu helped with the children and the cleaning. "Dinner's ready, dinner's ready," Muzit shouted, standing in the middle of the kitchen, still angry at her sister for not letting her wear my necklace. Ruth and Tamar pitched in to help Natzenet set the table.

"It's a little early for dinner, isn't it? Didn't you have a snack this afternoon?" I asked, looking at Tamar, while Ruth turned to the stove to check the food.

Senait had been playing with Muzit, but now she wanted me to carry her. Senait was the youngest, just five years old, and I enjoyed carrying her either on my back or in my arms; but I was a little tired that evening so I picked her up and gave her a squeeze, then placed her on a chair.

Mesfun left his desk to join us, and we all sat around the table ready to eat. Natzenet went to the maids' quarters to rest for a while and Shashu was downstairs ironing.

Just as we were about to say grace, we heard what sounded like fireworks. The noise got louder and louder, sounding more like guns, one bang after the other. Finally, there was a horrendous blast that seemed to rip through the earth and tear it in two. The girls screamed in terror and my heart raced. Poor Shashu came flying in like a bird. Natzenet walked in much more slowly, but she looked like a ghost.

We all ran to the family room and huddled together on the rug, hanging on to each other for dear life.

Mesfun, the only one among us who seemed to be in full control, stepped out through the kitchen door for a moment until I yelled at him to come back. He raised his eyebrows and gave me a very stern look for a moment; but when he saw how anxious I was for him, he came back and we held each other closely, involuntarily tightening our grip and rocking to and fro with each deafening mortar blast.

For an hour, there was not a moment's respite from the continuous roar of gunfire. Our fighters, our *tegadelti*, members of the Eritrean Liberation Front (ELF) and the Eritrean People's Liberation Front (EPLF), had attacked the military posts. The soldiers were returning fire aimlessly.

We all agreed that it would be a good idea to retreat to the storage room downstairs, but there was just one hitch: it would mean using the outside staircase. We eventually reasoned, however, that if the gunfire was aimed at our neighborhood at least some of the windows would have been shattered by that time, so we closed the kitchen door and headed down. Mesfun held Muzit and Tamar by the hand. Senait was on my back despite Natzenet's insistence that she carry her. Ruth took my hand and Natzenet was at my side. Shashu started out slowly but then she flew. The trek down the stairs took less than a minute but it seemed like an eternity.

The twelve-by-ten-foot storage room had no windows — just four walls and a small door. It was ideal as far as safety was concerned, but it was stuffy; we lasted only ten minutes before we all slipped out to Ruth's bedroom. Ruth was now amazingly unperturbed. Tamar seemed calm too, but there was a hint of uneasiness in her expressive eyes as they searched mine for assurance. Muzit, meanwhile, kept asking her father what was going on, while Senait was secure in my bosom. Shashu tried to hide her tears from us all, and Natzenet had a faraway look — she was thinking about her ten-year-old son who was living back in her village with her younger sister.

Finally, the sound of guns and mortar mercifully let up for a few minutes, giving us a moment to catch our breath. Mesfun and I took advantage of the opportunity to make frantic telephone calls to our families and friends. I glanced at the bedside clock. It was nine o'clock.

Again, one shell after the other rained down on the city, the vibration becoming ever more frightening. We were sure the building would cave in on top of us all. We squeezed each other tight while Mesfun did his best to calm everyone. Shashu wept openly now, and Natzenet scolded her for losing control in front of the children. Ruth and Tamar, in their embarrassment, offered faint smiles, and little Muzit, who loved Shashu dearly, was distressed by her tears. Senait, for her part, was by now nestled in my lap, feeling secure against the constant thunder overhead.

After a while, Mesfun stood up, straightened his pants, removed his tie, and sighed deeply. Don't worry, I'm here for you all, his smile seemed to convey. If we had been alone, nothing would have been more consoling to me than to throw myself into his arms. But how would the children feel if they saw me panic? I asked myself.

He eventually became restless and cautiously went outside and up the stairs. After much observation, he guessed that our fighters' cannons were aimed at the military installation with astonishing precision. The Ethiopian soldiers were retaliating rather aimlessly in the general direction of what they thought was the source of the shelling, Mesfun figured. The fire of the *tegadelti* was coming from the outskirts of Asmara as well as from inside the city itself.

The *tegadelti* were defying the great aggressors; they were attacking the invincible Ethiopian army right in their own bases! The very thought of it put a glow in my heart.

By midnight Muzit and Senait were both asleep, after Mesfun had managed to get to the kitchen and bring back something to eat. At one o'clock we were all drowsy; we pulled the mattresses from the beds onto the floor. Ruth and Tamar fell fast asleep in no time but neither Mesfun nor I could do more than doze. In my half-awake state, I could hear him getting up several times, pacing and opening the door gingerly.

The gunfire became more sporadic after midnight and subsided completely by half past five. At six o'clock the dawn glowed pink in the large windows, and with it came the joyful singing of birds.

At eight o'clock, while the others were still sleeping, Mesfun and I went upstairs and checked the rooms one by one. Then we cautiously opened the gate, and peered into the street. We were in a state of utter exhaustion from the long ordeal of the night, but we nonetheless felt the need to assure ourselves that the neighborhood was still in one piece.

On a normal Saturday, with no school, the children would already be out playing noisily; women would be off to the market in their horse-drawn carts; our neighbors would be out doing their chores — there would be all kinds of Saturday hustle and bustle.

But now we found the neighborhood completely deserted: not a soul had dared venture into the street. There was nothing but the incessant barking of dogs. It was as though they were protesting the bombardment of their city.

We left the eerie scene and returned to the comfort of home. "May the world be safe for you always," I murmured at the sight of my sleeping children. I was feeling my first doubts; the glow I had felt at the knowledge that our *tegadelti* were attacking the Dergue was being eclipsed by the realization that the government would surely retaliate. The inhabitants of the lowland areas in particular, and indeed people in many parts of Eritrea, had already suffered immeasurably at the hands of the Ethiopian military government, and now I had to face up to the fact that unspeakable atrocities could be committed against the civilian population of Asmara as well.

Natzenet and Shashu were up at half past eight, looking much better after a few hours sleep, and the girls awoke at ten. All were pleasantly surprised to see that the relentless roar of gunfire throughout the night had left our home unscathed; furthermore, the sun was out and the sky was still blue! We all hugged in celebration.

There was not enough bread to even get us through breakfast, and the previous night's casserole had been made from the week's leftovers. It was the end of the month and we had planned to do our monthly shopping that very day! When Ruth and Tamar opened the empty refrigerator they looked at me and I at them. There were only scraps from the night before.

Luckily, though, we had twenty pounds of wheat flour and two jars of jam, so Natzenet immediately started baking *kitcha*, our Eritrean unleavened bread. Tamar, Muzit, and Senait tore into the freshly-baked bread smothered with jam. Ruth laughed uneasily at how they were wolfing it down, but I was content to let them eat however they liked. God knows what tomorrow will bring, I thought.

The streets were empty that whole weekend, the first and second days of February. People who had been trapped in their places of work had to take whatever means they could to get to their homes, either in the city or in surrounding villages. By Monday, as many as four hundred had perished, according to some estimates, and there may have been more than that. Some were killed in the crossfire, but most, it was later revealed, were gunned down at random while passing the military bases as they tried to get home.

That week, the city was completely dead. Eritrean grocers, however, opened their back doors for two or three hours each day as a public service.

Our children's school, the Asmara International School, was closed, shattering Mesfun's dream — for this had been his pet project.

Originally started by British parents for their own children in the 1940s, the school had included a handful of American children by the 1960s. Since Mesfun was working for the American Consulate, the Vice-consul recommended him to the school board, and Ruth became the first Eritrean to go to the International School, starting out in kindergarten. By the 1970s, students of several other nationalities had been enrolled as well, and Mesfun had become the school's secretary-treasurer.

Since the teachers were all Americans and half the students were foreigners, it did not take long for the teachers and the parents to pack up and go home. The various expatriates trickled out of the country over the next month.

Two of my brothers and one sister came to stay with us for the time being. My parents' house in the Setanta Otto district of the city was close to a police station, and we were afraid that they would be mistaken for legadelti by the edgy policemen. There was Petros, the second oldest, who worked for my father's firm; Michael, at eighteen the youngest of the boys; and my sister Lia, the last of us nine children, who was only sixteen, a contemporary of our Ruth. My brother Dawit, the second youngest boy, refused to leave home. He wanted to be with our parents, come what may. Paulos, Demekesh, Solomon and Medhin were abroad for further studies.

I sensed that life in Asmara would never be the same. The capital's time had come for blood and terror.

It had not been the intention of our fighters to take over the city, nor could they have; they merely wanted to prove that they actually had the firepower to attack the Ethiopian military installation in Asmara, which was heavily fortified. After a week, they withdrew to an area that they could confidently defend.

The Ethiopian troops, unfortunately, had found a perfect opportunity to loot and kill shamelessly. In the first three days after the fighting broke out, the Ethiopian soldiers were afraid to budge from their posts, but then they literally became licensed thieves and murderers. It was a free-for-all. They would simply select homes and accuse the male occupants of being *shiftas* — bandits, as they called our *tegadelti*, and beat them, even killing some, taking whatever they wanted, from jewellery to cars to pots and pans.

Women and children were no less guilty in the eyes of the Dergue. The women were the mothers of the *tegadelti*, they reasoned, and the small children were future fighters. Yet through it all, the people of Asmara were happy to see that their sons and daughters had such determination and firepower and that one day, therefore, Eritrea would be free.

On Thursday, the sixth of February, Mesfun and I walked to Medhanie Alem Coptic Church, which was very close to our home. People had turned to the churches and the mosques; some families had even taken to sleeping in cathedrals, believing that the troops would not harm them there. Things had changed quite visibly around the church. There were no longer beggars sitting outside the gate, the small trees inside the compound looked limp, and the church door was closed. Mesfun went to join a small group of men chatting in a circle in the churchyard.

I looked for a familiar face among the several groups of women. My eye caught sight of a woman I knew from the neighborhood, with whom I had always exchanged greetings. She was speaking loudly and harshly, with one hand on her waist and the other cutting through the air. Saliva had gathered in the corners of her mouth and her lips were dry and parched. Her eyes were devoid of life.

"What is going on?" I asked.

"What do you think I'm doing?" this once serene and pleasant woman asked with a tone that was sharp and decidedly hostile.

"I don't know. My husband and I came to pray and to see

how everyone is making out," I replied. She had to struggle to swallow her saliva and with a distraught voice continued:

"I don't think I have a husband any more, my friend. Many of his workmates made it home — one died and was buried yesterday. My son left home two days ago to find his father and he still hasn't come back. I don't think I'm ever going to see either one of them ever again. I only hope I'm wrong. Do you have any idea where they could be?" She looked straight into my eyes.

It was only then that I realized the poor woman had gone out of her mind. She looked as though she had neither eaten nor slept for days; it had all been too much for her to bear. The sight of this woman's desperation was devastating to me. What could I say? At any rate, she didn't wait for my answer. She locked her hands behind her back and began wandering aimlessly about the churchyard.

A priest came to open the church and Mesfun fetched me to go in for the service, but I was so shaken that I wanted only to go home. I needed to be alone, I needed to think. The plight of this poor woman had brought home to me the unspeakable crimes being perpetrated against my people.

"Don't take everything to heart," said Mesfun when I told him about the woman whose family was missing. "Be strong, my dear, be strong."

When we got back to the house, everyone but Petros was downstairs. Ruth, Micael, Tamar, and Lia were playing cards; Muzit was listening to music; Shashu was pushing Senait on the swing. Their comfortable little world was still safe. I wasn't in the mood to talk to the children. Petros came down and he and Mesfun immediately got into a conversation about the war.

I went up to the family room and sat on the sofa to gaze at the picture of the horses that had always given me peace, but it did not help. I went to the living room and tried in vain to water the plants. I went to the bedroom and lay down to think, but I felt only a huge vacuum inside of me. Just as I was about to kneel and force myself to pray, Shashu came in holding Senait by the hand. Amazingly, the emptiness suddenly disappeared. My Senait became my solace. How comforting it was to cradle her in my arms, even though she was getting too big for that. Shashu noticed that I wanted to be alone with my baby and graciously took leave, closing the door behind her. Suddenly I started shedding tears, tears of pain and anguish, and at the same time tears of comfort.

"Why are you crying, Mommy?" Senait asked.

"My eyes hurt — maybe I'm catching a cold," I replied quickly, wiping away the tears.

When we joined the rest of the family, Muzit was still listening to her music. Being a very sensitive child, she noticed that I didn't look right and gave me such a big hug that I cherish it to this day. I sat on the sofa with both girls on my lap.

Ruth and Tamar were absorbed in their card game with Michael and Lia. "Hi, Mommy. Guess what — I'm winning!" gloated Tamar. "I wouldn't brag if I were you," Lia said. "It's your turn again."

Ruth saw that I was upset but was compelled to continue playing. "When we're through with this game, Mommy, come and join in," she pleaded. But I declined and they continued their game in high spirits. How the four of them have grown recently, I thought — Michael and Lia as well as Ruth and Tamar.

Mesfun and Petros were at another table having their own game of cards. Petros, our contact with the front, was whistling away. I couldn't wait to get his news from the field.

When I did hear Petros' news from the front, it was indeed good, and it managed to perk me up considerably. Dinner was served late and afterward we listened to the BBC, but Eritrea was not mentioned. We had just about given up all hope of hearing anything on Voice of America, but we kept trying every evening, nonetheless. All we could expect to get from the government-owned Ethiopian National Radio and its Asmara branch was propaganda. The atrocities committed by the troops were never reported.

For the first two weeks after the open fighting had begun on the thirty-first of January we stayed at home with our family, just as everyone did. We ventured out only to go to church and to shop for food. Then most government offices, businesses, and factories reopened, and Mesfun and I went back to our jobs.

It was finally confirmed, however, that the doors of the Asmara International School would be closed permanently, to Mesfun's bitter disappointment, so we hired an Eritrean woman to come to our home on a part-time basis and teach the children mathematics and written Tigrinya, our language.

Natzenet, meanwhile, decided to leave the country and went to Beirut to work for a Lebanese family. I was very sorry to lose such a good housekeeper, but I knew that she would at least be safe. Natzenet's departure brought more household responsibilities to Ruth and Tamar; they enjoyed it at first, but the novelty of the job soon wore off.

As the days progressed, Mesfun and I could see that our daughters' confinement to their home, even with a tutor, was no fun for them. Ruth, who loved to read, continued to do so, but without her usual enthusiasm. The always joking and giggling Tamar grew more reserved. The free-spirited and exuberant Muzit was not herself at all. She adored watching the sun rise and set and had been in the habit of bringing others along to share her excitement, but now she sat on the steps to watch all alone — she seemed to be questioning the heavens as to what was going on. I had thought at first that Senait did not understand much, but the way she hugged us when we came home from work each evening told me that not even my little one was untouched by Eritrea's troubles.

When guests came to visit or to stay the night, the girls hated for them to leave. They fretted about their inevitable departure almost as soon as the visitors were in the door. Our country's political situation was taking its toll on our children.

When the public schools reopened after a few months, therefore, we enrolled the girls at Comboni College, where my brother Michael attended. Most of the students at Comboni were Eritreans, and although this hardly fazed Muzit and Senait, it was a totally new world for Ruth and Tamar. My sister Lia, who also had been at the Asmara International School, now went to Comboni as well.

Lia and Michael had long since returned home to my parents' house.

For his part, Petros narrowly escaped death at the hands of the *afagn* and fled Asmara to fight with the EPLF.

The Dergue, meanwhile, had a massive public relations job on its hands; it had to convince the outside world that Asmara was still a peaceful place. The consulates remained open until early 1976, albeit with skeleton staffs. But marshal law continued and the seven p.m. to six a.m. curfew was never lifted. In fact, people tended to be home long before seven o'clock; the customary evening stroll and window shopping along the broad avenues had become a thing of the past.

A black cloud hung over the entire city. Government offices and major businesses, like banks and airlines, were heavily guarded. The soldiers posted on every corner appeared tense and bewildered. The beautiful and once wonderfully light-hearted Asmara was mute and deserted by five p.m. Many low-income families picked up and went to stay with relatives in the countryside, while others from the villages where fighting had taken place streamed into the capital. Everywhere there was uneasiness and fear; yet one could also detect a sense of hope in the air.

Five months passed, and still the fighting continued in the villages surrounding Asmara. The Ethiopian army lost one battle after another. And every time they were whipped by our *tegadelti* they unleashed their anger on innocent civilians.

Many highlanders — men, women, and children — crossed the Eritrean border to Sudan to live a miserable existence as refugees, as had their brothers and sisters from the lowlands where the resistance movement had taken root a decade before.

It was at this time that young boys and girls, most of them of high-school age, joined the fronts in such large numbers that many had to be turned away. Mothers actively encouraged their children to go. It was better to fight for a worthy cause, the parents reasoned, and face death with their brothers and sisters in struggle, than stay home and hope to evade the wolves.

A week or so after the fighting had ceased in Asmara and the *tegadelti* had withdrawn to areas that they could easily defend, the underground movement became more active and organized. Thousands of residents of Asmara, men and women, girls and boys, joined small, clandestine groups called *cells* of no more than seven members each. Day in and day out, government bureaucrats, office workers, accountants, medical doctors, nurses, health officers, engineers, electricians, mechanics, teachers, technicians, and truck drivers joined the resistance, and they brought with them valuable information, documents, technical know-how, hospital equipment, medicine, and money. Students with university degrees from both East and West streamed into the Eritrean mountains through Sudan, mostly to the EPLF: which gradually emerged as the strongest resistance movement.

Cooperation between the city-dwelling underground members and the actual fighters was exemplary. They were so highly organized, and their operations were so perfectly synchronised, that our *tegadelti* usually managed to accomplish their missions in Asmara and get back to their bases without firing a shot.

The Dergue was so humiliated by the intelligence, courage, and commitment of the *tegadelti* — and, worse, the cooperation that they had come to expect from the Eritrean public — that they resorted to indiscriminate imprisonment and torture.

# Three

When I was pushed into the cell by the guard, it was very dark. At first I could barely make out the blurred outlines of human forms, but then slowly I began to see eyes, heads, faces, hands, and finally human beings — women.

"Dear sister, please sit down," said a young woman, pointing to a folded blanket in the corner of the tiny, six-by-five-foot cell.

"Welcome, and try to calm down — please," said another, who was sitting with her knees tucked under her chin and her hands locked around them.

"I'm lucky to be with you... and not alone," I ventured.

One of them sat close to me and whispered in my ear. "The name of the game is deny. Never admit to anything. Never! Even if they crucify you."

"I don't think there'll be any interrogation for you tonight," said another of the women. "Let's hope and pray your interrogator won't be Luul — that demon. He'll pay for it dearly one day!"

The cellmate who had whispered in my ear wanted to know who I was and what part of the city I was from. It turned out that three of them knew me by name, and for a moment there was heavy silence.

"Her too — those bastards," a woman lying on the floor muttered bitterly.

My cellmate with her knees drawn up to her chin was eager to find out if I knew her husband. All of them, of course, were anxious to know what was going on in town and the latest news about our *tegadelti*. I was not sure who the woman's husband was, and I did not want to say much about anything except to thank them for the advice they were giving me and for their concern.

Interrogator... demon... denial... pray.

I was trying to analyze everything: why I was there. It had not yet registered that I was under lock and key.

The imposing palace, one of the most impressive buildings in Asmara, had been built by the Italians as a governor's residence. It had included offices, servants' quarters, a large compound with horse stables and tracks, and a small zoo. When the British took over, they used the palace as the department of education. Under Ethiopian rule, it became the residence of Emperor Haile Selassie's representative.

After the overthrow of the Emperor in 1974, the new Ethiopian military régime, the Dergue, used most of the compound for offices and converted the three large stables into a prison. While two stables were left as is to hold as many prisoners as possible, the third, in the middle, was divided by concrete walls into several cells — an equal number on each side with a corridor in the center. The cell into which I was thrown was the second from the rear on the right.

The five women unfolded their blankets to cover the entire floor and did their best to squeeze together so that I would have enough space to lie down.

But I slept not a wink the whole night.

Why did the driver and his companion rush away after they dumped me at the prison? I wondered. Could they have gone back to the airline office to check my private papers? Where's that list of the twenty or so women villagers who were getting help from the YWCA? It's in my handbag. My Lord! It is perfectly innocuous, but it could easily be misconstrued.... My mind was feverish, jumping from one frightening thought to the next.... If they search our house and find copies of *Mahta*, the EPLF newsletter, it will destroy us all!... My friends at the office would surely have contacted Mesfun immediately, and surely he's wise enough to take care of it.... If the *afagn* burst into the house and mistreat Mesfun in front of the children.... my God... how will it affect them?

Finally I heard a cock crow. The thirtieth of September had given way to the first of October — one whole night in prison; one whole night without enough air to breathe; one whole night on a hard floor with five women I had never laid eyes on in my entire life, squashed together like six sardines in a tin.

But I still wanted to believe it was all a dream.... I felt I heard my children coming up the stairs, knocking on the bedroom door, kissing their father and falling all over me.... I selected a dress from my wardrobe and put it on.... I could almost feel myself jumping up and running out and getting into our car.

But there I was in a cell without room to budge an inch, much less turn over. And there was a heavy iron door that was locked from the outside. It began to dawn on me that I was under arrest at the Palace Prison! I was only a ten-minute drive from my home, yet I felt I was miles and miles away, out of touch, out of reach. Being a mother, going to work, having friends over — these simple pleasures would now be history. My life was no longer my own. I had lost my freedom as a human being and my rights as a citizen. My very life was in danger. I was now sharing the fate of countless thousands of other Eritreans.

Still in a state of inner turmoil... arguing... explaining... struggling in my mind with my captors, I said "Good morning" to my cellmates and forced a thin smile. Understanding the great effort it took to fake even the weakest of greetings, no doubt remembering their own agonising first night in prison, they could not help but weep. The evening before they had put on a brave front; now, however briefly, they seemed to be reliving the pain. I could hold back my anguish no longer. Hot tears flushed down my cheeks.

Soon the door swung open noisely and we were told by a guard to go to the outside toilets immediately.

And a toilet it was. There was — thankfully — a roof, but the four walls consisted of corrugated tin sheets hastily thrown together. A hole had been cut in the centre of the concrete floor, and the floor was so completely covered with human feces that I found it next to impossible to get enough space to plant my two feet and squat. The sight and the smell were gut-wrenching. Given some water, the prisoners would have been delighted to clean the place, but of course it was intended as a form of humiliation.

We were then allowed to wash our hands and faces from a faucet on the outside wall of the building in the open air before being escorted back to our cell.

As soon as we returned, my cellmates offered me a piece of bread and a half cup of tea from a thermos sent from one of their homes, but I had no appetite whatsoever; not even a drop of water could have passed through my parched lips.

At nine o'clock I began to hear cars arriving and people talking. The daily chores of the jailers had begun. It was time to start the first round of interrogation for that day. The names of two men were called... and then my heart skipped a beat, for I heard my own name. There was time for only a quick prayer and a few kind words of encouragement from my cellmates before a guard unlocked our cell door, threw it open wide, and shouted, "Prisoner Abeba, come out!"

I followed him to the interrogation room, which was located some thirty yards from our cell and adjacent to the office of the Major — the warden of the Palace Prison.

The room was small and rectangular with a mean little window, a hard concrete floor, and bare walls. My two interrogators, seated casually on wooden chairs behind a table — the chairs and the table were the only furniture in the room — motioned for me to sit on the chair provided for the prisoner. One of them was a young man of about twenty-eight; he had closely cropped hair and his bright red shirt and brown jacket clashed violently before my tired eyes. He was clearly trying to effect the demeanor of an educated and sophisticated man, but just as clearly to me he was neither. The other interrogator, who may have been in his early forties, was dressed in khaki and could easily have passed for a janitor in a government building.

The older man proceeded: "Do you know where you are?"

What an absurd question, I thought, but answered, "Yes."

"Do you know that you have to tell the truth here?"

"I know that one should tell the truth always, everywhere," I replied firmly.

They both nodded their heads and there was a moment of silence. Then the older of the two wrote down my name and personal particulars.

Suddenly the young man pushed back his chair and slowly and deliberately he got up. He stood about three feet away from me and casually asked:

"How was your first night in detention?" It was as though

we were at a cocktail party and he was asking, How did you enjoy the opera?

"It was terrible," I replied.

He cleared his throat and walked back to his chair, then continued:

"You have been under suspicion for a long time, and now we have documented evidence as well as witnesses. You have definitely made a mistake, but it is a mistake that can be pardoned. One night in prison is already too much — 'terrible,' as you say. However, if you confess what we already know, we will write it all down for you and all you have to do is sign. Once you confess, the government will pardon you — meaning you can resume your normal life. After all, you are the mother of four children and we don't want them to suffer."

He started to smile, and his fellow interrogator began putting pen to paper. They were waiting for me to start.

I drew a deep breath.

"Gentlemen, I am at a complete loss," I said. "I don't know why I am here and I don't know what you are talking about. I can't tell you what I don't know. I have never consciously harmed anyone, and it therefore goes without saying that I have no confession to make."

The atmosphere changed palpably. The two frowned ferociously and shouted almost in unison:

"Woman!"

Then the younger man kept quiet while his partner resumed:

"You look like life has been fair to you — and we have been fair too. Have we not been nice? But if you choose to play games with us, we will show you another side — you can be sure of that....How dare you act innocent and plead ignorance when you are a staunch supporter of the so-called freedom fighters!"

There was no response from me.

"Speak, woman, speak!"

Both their faces contorted into ugly snarls.

"I still do not understand what you are talking about," I replied, fighting very hard to keep control.

"Guard! Guard!" the young interrogator roared. "Take this fool back to her cell. She has one more night to think it over."

He grabbed my shoulder roughly and shoved me out of the interrogation room through the half-open door. I was seized with outrage; I felt like fighting back physically. But I managed to get hold of myself.

Being humiliated by these thugs cannot hurt me, I thought. They have flesh but no soul, guns but no guts.

My cell, which had been the shock of my life a mere sixteen hours before, looked beautiful to me now. True, it was the same windowless, airless room, just six feet long by five feet wide; but after spending time in the interrogation room with the two brutes, it was heaven to be back with the women. They were people like myself, born and reared in the same land, doomed to the same fate, and cut off from the world for the same reason.

My whole outlook began to change. I thanked the Lord for giving me such wonderful cellmates as Semhar, Fana, Ribka, Tsegga, and Saba. I would handle whatever interrogations lay in store for me, I vowed, and I would bear whatever physical pain might be inflicted upon me.

The Dergue did not provide prisoners with food. We were entirely dependent on our families and friends for our meals. Food parcels were collected quite a distance from the prison grounds, checked by the guards, and transported to the prison between noon and one in the afternoon. Distribution was made by roll call: all the cell doors were opened at once and left slightly ajar; when your name was called, you tapped lightly on the door of your cell and replied "Present" or "Here"; then you were given your food parcel from home.

That afternoon, I received my first food parcel from my family, and they had included two sets of underwear, a dress, one blanket, and one sheet.

Then everything that had transpired the previous day came to mind — the special hugs I had given my children, the excitement I had felt cutting and arranging the flowers for the table, the wonderful lunch with our guests, the way I was forced to leave my office, stepping in the *afagn* car at gunpoint, the deathly silence while I was driven around the city.

I thought of how my children would take the news of my imprisonment, and of how the afagn might burst into our home and search through our papers, throwing open doors and dresser drawers and scattering about all our precious belongings. I started feeling sad and depressed, but then I quickly perked up. For I had learned something about myself — that even though I could get extraordinarily furious or extraordinarily sad, I had the power to keep these strong emotions under control.

I thought of how lucky I was to even be within the walls of the prison. So many Eritreans left their homes and places of work just the way I had, and never made it to prison. They were shot or beaten to death, or stabbed, strangled with piano wire. Sometimes, families had no clue whatsoever for months when people were spirited away like I was. They had to live with the uncertainty of not knowing if their loved ones were dead or left to rot in some prison.

There was certainly no guarantee that once you were imprisoned you were out of danger — I had no delusions about that — but there was a good chance of having the benefit of a trial, and of surviving, I assured myself.

It is amazing how your thinking can drastically change within hours, minutes, even seconds, when you are suddenly faced with the stark reality of imprisonment, torture, or even death.

# Four

September, the beginning of our new year, is perhaps the very best month in Eritrea. In the countryside, the fields of grain are ripe. The mountains, hills, and plains are covered with wild daisies and tall grass. The early morning sunshine on the beautiful hills and plains is breathtaking.

During the first five days of September, we celebrate a holiday called *Pagumen*. Women, girls, and young boys flock to the lakes and ponds near their homes to bathe. To me, it symbolises the washing away of one year and the welcoming of the new with both clean body and clean soul. Before and after bathing, the girls sing and dance. This celebration is much more intense in the countryside than in the cities, and it is a great occasion for young boys and girls to meet.

It was during *Pagumen* in the village of Beleza, about five miles from Asmara, that Abraha met Wuba, my cellmate, Semhar's mother. Abraha's younger brother, who normally brought their cattle to pasture and tended them, was sent on an errand to a nearby village. Abraha therefore took the herd to the fields for grazing. On the way he met a group of five girls returning home after bathing, and his eyes met Wuba's. Strange feelings crept over Wuba, but she had no idea what they were. Abraha, though, a boy of seventeen, knew what was happening when his heart started pounding. He began to follow her secretly and watch her while she was drawing water from the well, and while she was playing with her friends outside her home.

Finally, Abraha's sleepless nights and absent-mindedness gave him away.

"What's wrong with you, lad?" asked his father. "Who's the girl you're daydreaming about?"

So he knows, thought the embarrassed Abraha, and before he could stop himself, the name "Wuba" slipped out of his mouth.

The father was extremely happy, for he had already been thinking of looking for a girl for his son. He knew Wuba's parents well — they were highly respected and wealthy, and they were from the same village. Who wouldn't want to betroth his son to a wealthy family? Then the boy's family gets a substantial dowry. Woe to the girl whose parents could not afford a dowry — finding a husband for her was not easy.

The money and the cattle that Wuba brought as her dowry helped the couple to live a reasonably good life for five years; but the lot of the farmer was not easy and Abraha's case was no exception. He left the land and found a job in Asmara as a laborer for a construction company, at the minimum wage of a dollar a day. At first he enjoyed the bicycle ride to town and back, but then the daily commuting began to wear him down, so Abraha decided to move his family to Asmara and leave his house and farm to the care of his parents and his neighbors.

By the time they had moved to Asmara and settled into a small rental house in the Abashawul area, Semhar and her two brothers had been born and Abraha's father had died. The adjustment from farm life to city life was rough. Abraha labored to provide a better life for his family, but he could not earn more than a dollar and fifty cents a day. Over the following few years, two more boys were born, which meant that Wuba and Abraha had two more mouths to feed. Then, while working outdoors one cold morning, Abraha got pneumonia; he died at the age of thirty-one.

His wife was left penniless, with five children to rear, Semhar being the eldest at ten years of age. With twenty-five dollars in capital, Wuba and her daughter went into business. They bought small quantities of tomatoes and onions from farmers and sold them in the local market. This way, they could at least scrape together the five dollars a month for their room and have one meagre meal a day. The next two children were compelled to contribute to the family income by carrying sacks of grain and vegetables for women as they walked home from the market, for a wage of a few cents and a piece of bread each trip.

So with a penny here and a penny there, the family managed to survive, and even to send the fourth child to school.

Semhar recalled to me how the whole family was bursting with excitement the day he started school, wearing his new clothes and carrying his notebook and his pencil. On that historic day, she overheard her mother giving a soliloquy to her departed father:

"If you hadn't wandered from place to place enduring the cold of morning and the heat of midday looking for menial jobs; if you hadn't worked so hard as a stone cutter, for so little; if your pride hadn't been wounded because you couldn't support your family to your liking; if you had stayed in the hospital when you were sick, you would be alive today to see your son going to school. You never failed me, Abraha, and I will never fail you. May your spirit rest in peace."

The whole family continued to struggle for a living. The lucky brother made it to the fifth grade, while Semhar herself learned the alphabet and simple arithmetic at an uncertified neighborhood school. The two older boys also went to the neighborhood school; as they grew older they were able to carry heavier loads and therefore earn a little more for the family.

Semhar grew up to be a beautiful girl. Her mother was confident that someone would ask for her daughter's hand; her worry was how on earth would she get the money for a dowry. Semhar herself knew that it would not be easy to find a husband — and the lack of a dowry was not the only reason. The other was that no longer was Semhar the shy, obedient village girl that she was expected to be; the rough life of the market had made her independent and tough. She was too independent for rural suitors, yet too uncultured and at the same time too independent for city boys. At any rate, even if by some chance she was fortunate enough to find a mate, Semhar had made a secret vow that she would never get married until her younger brothers were grown and able to support themselves and their mother without her help.

Semhar would wake up early in the morning, she recounted, fetch water from the community well, sweep the room, and get her brother ready for school. He was the only boy to have an extra pair of pants and a second shirt and to get a piece of bread and a small cup of tea for breakfast. The rest of the family had only one meal a day — dinner — which consisted of *engera* and *tsebhi*.

Evening was the best time of the day. Wuba would sit and rest after her hard day's work, while the children studied. They read aloud and practised writing on scraps of paper collected from the streets. The three-year-old would make sounds, imitating his brothers' reading. There were no chairs in the house. Their only possessions were two beds, three benches, a table, a few pots and pans, a charcoal stove, an oil lamp, a wooden box for their few treasures, and a five-by-three-inch mirror on the wall alongside photographs cut from newspapers.

The mother would tell them stories of her childhood and youth — about the sheep, goats, cattle, and oxen her parents had, and how she loved to milk the goats. She told them about being married at the age of twelve and about how she cried desperately for months to go back to her parents, upsetting the poor bridegroom — their father — and her in-laws. Her embarrassed husband spent the first three months of their marriage coaxing her into staying by sneaking to Asmara to buy her candy. The children would roar with laughter. They could not picture their mother crying and being comforted by candy, just like a baby.

The boy who went to the government school would tell stories about his day, and the two older boys shared anecdotes about their customers — the good-hearted ones who in addition to the agreed payment would give them a nice chunk of bread and tea; and the mean ones who would coldly hand them their pay. They talked about the part-time community school and the gossip of the marketplace. The impoverished but happy family was the envy of all the neighbors. But their harmonious family life was brought to an abrupt halt when the youngest child died of diarrhea and dysentery. Wuba was inconsolable. The dead child had been the last fruit of the man who had struggled so hard to provide for his family. Only their fierce closeness helped the family to eventually get over their grief.

One day a gunshot pierced through the market stalls where the whole family made its living. Armed soldiers appeared at once and randomly picked out a carload of people to be carted off to prison. Among them was Semhar.

At the *ghebi* prison — the Palace Prison — the interrogators used their dreaded "number eight" torture on Semhar. Her big toes were tied together with rope and her arms were forced around her legs; then she was hung upside down so that her body formed a figure eight. They inserted a piece of wood between her teeth and beat her mercilessly on the soles of her feet with a rubber truncheon. They repeated the torture, demanding that she confess. But Semhar had no confession to make. She had not the faintest idea what the incident in the market had been all about.

When I arrived in the cell, two months had elapsed since Semhar's last beating. She still felt pain in the evenings, especially when it was cold, although she was determined to conceal it from the rest of us. She was constantly talking about her brothers and her devoted mother. "If you could see her act the peacemaker in the market squabbles, you would be amazed. Mother's face never used to show misery at all. It was only after we lost my brother that she changed; then her grief left her face permanently lined." Then Semhar's tone changed: "And now, thanks to these *deki sheramuth* [sons of whores], my being thrown in jail will probably finish the poor woman off."

Semhar was imprisoned for four months without a trial. She received food parcels from her mother and their friends during her first three weeks in prison, but then the meals stopped and for several weeks there was no news at all from her family. A week before my arrival, however, she received a parcel. On the back of the box it read "From Mother," and below this were the signatures of her three brothers. This made her day and many more after that.

Just as vivacious Semhar had been the life of her family, she was also a great source of laughter and entertainment in our little cell. I am sure that if she had had the benefit of an education, she would have accomplished much.

Fana was a quiet, heavy-set woman of medium height in her early thirties. She usually wore a shawl around her shoulders, and on her face there was nearly always the same disturbed expression. Life had not been fair to Fana, who was originally from Decamare, a town twenty-five miles south of Asmara. She had a relative who had become a teacher after finishing sixth grade, and this woman had been Fana's idol. Not many girls in Decamare went to school when Fana was a child, and those who finished the sixth grade and became teachers — were very few indeed. Fana's dream was to be a teacher like her relative. But her parents had other plans: Their dream was to find Fana a good husband from a good family, and marry her off.

In the old days, arranged marriages worked beautifully most of the time. The couple would not meet until their wedding day, and only after the priest or the elders pronounced them husband and wife would they get to know each other. Later, they would fall in love or simply live together, usually developing an attachment as they brought up their family. There was no such thing as falling in love and getting married, as is customary in the West.

In arranged marriages, a middleman, the matchmaker, plays an important role. It is he who determines the compatibility of the families. Either he initiates the idea and shares it with the father of the boy, or the boy's father approaches him. The father of the boy inquires about the reputation of the girl's family — their integrity, social status, physical and mental health. Most important of all, he wants to know whether the mother of the girl is a hard worker and a good homemaker, and whether she respects and reveres her husband, for it is believed that the daughter takes after the mother.

Then the matchmaker approaches the father of the girl, who asks similar questions. When the girl's father, who might consult his uncles, perhaps some cousins and an elder, decides that the family is worthy and that the boy is strong and healthy, he gives a signal to the matchmaker that he is at least interested.

The mothers of both parties are included in the selection of the spouse, but always behind the scenes.

Even though a decision may have already been taken within the girl's family, her father does not accept the proposal for his daughter's hand right away. The boy's father must first court the entire family.

Fana suspected that the four men who came to speak with her father every two weeks, very early in the mornings, were up to something. She was not happy when the prospective in-laws brought her new clothes and a small cross on a chain, a symbol of engagement. The girl to be betrothed was never asked her opinion, and it was unthinkable for her to go against the wishes of her parents. Fana was engaged at the age of thirteen, and her schooling came to an abrupt end. She had completed the fourth grade. She was married when she was fourteen years old. The strong-willed Fana was furious but she could not allow herself the luxury of venting her anger at her parents or at society at large — it was the tradition, after all, and very few girls rebelled against it.

Fana was not lucky enough to fall in love or develop a close relationship with her husband. The longer she stayed with her husband, the more unbearable it became. Rare were the nights that he would leave her alone on her side of the bed to drift off to sleep in peace. Fana could tell just by the look in his eyes over dinner whether they were going to have sex that night. He would simply blow out the kerosene lamp, grab his wife, pull off her clothes, and force himself on her. Then she was obliged to rub his back and soothe him to sleep in order that he be completely serviced. What is meant to be a sacred and beautiful experience was terrifying and repulsive to Fana, and she came to dread the close of the day for fear of what lay in store for her.

She would feel used and abused after every one of these assaults, but she had no one in whom to confide. It was unacceptable for a wife to complain to her parents or the village elders about her marriage unless the husband squandered his money or was unfaithful to her. Sexual behavior and sexual problems were taboo as subjects for discussion by women; but for Fana, sleeping with her husband was not lovemaking at all — she saw it as nothing but rape.

After four years of this mistreatment, the eighteen-year-old Fana just walked away and disappeared one morning after her husband had gone to work. The family spent ten days frantically searching for her, and finally her aunt found her at the home of a friend in a nearby village.

"If you keep on begging me to go back to him, I'll go away and you'll never see me again — not ever," Fana told her parents. They had no choice but to give in. Her mother was crushed — she wanted her daughter to give her many grandchildren. Since Fana had no children or valuable property, divorce was easily obtained. The rejected husband wasted no time in finding another woman and remarrying.

Fana went back to her parents' home, but six months later she decided that she would move to Asmara and begin a new life. If she lived much longer with her parents, she feared, it was inevitable that men would ask her to marry for a second time, the thought of which repelled her.

She could have gone back to school and become a teacher, but during the four years of Fana's marriage, many changes had taken place. Girls now had to finish eighth grade before becoming teachers. Besides, Fana was uncomfortable with the idea of returning to the classroom. She felt too old.

When Fana left Decamare with the little money that her parents had given her to start out, it was with ambivalent feelings. She hoped that Asmara would offer her the chance of a better life; yet she was uneasy, for she had never been on her own before.

With little education and no skills, Fana found it impossible to find a well-paying job, but she eventually found work as a laborer in a sack factory at minimum wage, and she moved in with a friend of a relative. She barely managed to pay her share of the rent and to feed and clothe herself. This was not the life that the ambitious and enlightened Fana had envisioned.

The moment the Ethiopian government set foot in Eritrea, they began to subtly erode the high standard of education set by the British administration and encouraged the proliferation of bars where imported hard liquor is sold, *mies* and *sewa* houses, and brothels. *Mies* and *sewa* are indigenous drinks, the first made from honey and herbs and the latter from barley and sorghum. It became fashionable to frequent drinking establishments, and sexual exploitation and corruption followed closely behind. .

Women bar owners and bartenders did very well for themselves financially under these conditions. They could afford to buy expensive clothes and luxurious houses. Some of them even had their own cars. Moreover, these women were very much respected by the government. They would be invited to the palace for grand occasions such as the Emperor's birthday.

For a woman like Fana, who had great ambitions the bar business looked very attractive indeed. So after five years she quit her job at the sack factory and was taken on as a bar maid.

After only two years, with the help of friends and relatives, Fana managed to raise enough money to buy her own bar. Her business thrived. The iron-willed Fana believed she could take care of herself any time, anywhere, but it wasn't long before the young woman learned that it was next to impossible to be in the bar business and remain pure. She would feel very hurt when a man who she would not even consider fit to talk to would ask her to be his "special friend" — to sleep with him.

After a while, Fana came to long for a husband and children. Bar women, however, did not have a good reputation and the chances of getting marriage proposals were slim. The more Fana looked for the husband of her dreams, the more discouraged she became.

At times Fana thought God was punishing her for leaving her husband. But she reasoned that she was young at the time and that her spouse had not even been of her own choice. Had she been more mature, she thought, perhaps she could have salvaged the marriage — always blaming herself for the fiasco.

Then, when she was approaching the age of thirty, a man five years her senior who had occasionally patronized her bar discovered the real Fana — not a public entertainer, not a gold-digger, but a loving and caring woman who desperately wanted to make a home. When he placed an engagement ring on her finger, Fana felt she was being crowned queen of the world!

Fana was married without fanfare in the Asmara municipal office. Her husband moved into her home, and since he owned a small business, she sold her bar in order to take on the job of full-time wife. Eritreans strongly believe in helping their parents, and Fana contributed financially to the well-being of her parents and her siblings, adding two rooms to her parents' tiny house. To her mother, though, nothing could equal the joy of seeing her daughter as a respectable homemaker.

A year later she gave birth to a baby boy. A baptism in the Christian Orthodox faith is a very festive event, and since the couple had invited no one to their wedding. this was planned as a celebration for both occasions.

Fana bought a special outfit. She had taken to dressing up both herself and the baby, sitting in front of the mirror to admire the beautiful picture. She would then imagine the long-awaited event.

Three days before the celebration, when all the guests had been invited and preparations were in full swing, two jeeps filled with what seemed like Gestapo officers surrounded their house. Fana was breast-feeding her baby when three men burst through the door, ordered her to put the infant in his crib, and with a machine gun pointed at her back forced her out of the house. They brought her to the Carchelli Prison downtown.

She had not gone two steps into the interrogation room when belts, sticks, and rubber truncheons assaulted her entire body, especially her back and shoulders. Fana could not figure out what was going on. It had all happened in less than forty minutes: the breaking in of her front door with a deafening crash, the hasty departure, the drive to the prison amidst armed soldiers, and then the savage beating.

The shock was unbearable. Fana fell unconscious and was left for dead in the interrogation room overnight. But her strong heart refused to give up. The head of Carchelli Prison was dumbfounded when he was told that she had survived the night. Then Fana was moved to a cell. As she regained consciousness the pain became more acute; her dress, which had become glued to her body by the blood from the beating, peeled off her skin at the slightest movement. The pain was compounded by Fana's longing to hold and nurse her newborn.

Four days later, two prisoners were thrown in with Fana. After staying a month in *Carchelli*, she was transferred to the Palace Prison. It was her second week there when I joined them. Her interrogation was resumed at the Palace, but there were no further physical attacks.

It turned out that during her business days, an Ethiopian army officer had wanted to share Fana's bed and had been rejected. He had asked her to marry him, and she had again turned him down. But the man did not give up easily. While he was doing his best to win her over, he was sent to Ethiopia on a mission. On his return, he was furious to find out that she had married an Eritrean. Fana was charged with letting *tegadelti* patronize her bar and passing along to them information that she had allegedly picked up from her Ethiopian customers. No evidence was necessary and the officer's word was proof enough. His revenge was complete.

As the days went by her wounds began to heal, but being deprived of her infant son was not easy. Later she was seized by a new fear: "Will my baby know me when I get out? What about my husband? Will he find another woman?" She was a bar woman, after all. Fana's anxiety was a frightening thing to watch. When she sat with her knees drawn up to her chin, just as she had the first time I saw her, I could literally feel her pain.

Three days in prison. I almost got used to the routine: wake up early, fold the blankets, sweep the few feet of floor with a tiny broom, (how it made its way into the cell I have no idea), visit the toilets, receive parcels from home, try to identify the movements in the corridor (whether it be guards or prisoners), and pray every time a prisoner was called for interrogation.

Toilet visits were twice a day — early in the morning and between half past four and half past five in the afternoon. In the morning, the guards always rushed us. The afternoons were more relaxed. Once in a while, they even left us to wash our hands from the faucets in the compound that the men were using; talking, however, was strictly forbidden.

The first time I visited the toilet, Fana walked close to me and whispered, "Don't think everybody in the cell is a true Eritrean." I was taken aback. "Be careful of Ribka and Tsegga. They might tell you stories about themselves and their heroism as underground ELF members in Asmara. Yes, sure, at one time they were, but no longer."

Fana checked to make sure no one was watching, then she went on in a conspiratorial tone: "Now they're spies for the Amharas [the inhabitants of certain Ethiopian provinces are Amhara, but the term is used pejoratively to mean members of the ethnic ruling class]. Every prisoner knows about these sluts. They incriminated three men." Without waiting for my reaction, Fana quickened her pace and walked on. She said nothing more.

I was puzzled by this incident. When I had first met my cellmates, they seemed a united group. Fana's information disturbed me.

On the morning of my fourth day in prison, Ribka asked me to skip the afternoon toilet visit. If she is a spy, I thought, I cannot believe she would be that open. I prepared myself, in case she had any tricky questions planned. When the guard opened the door for the afternoon toilet visit and Semhar said, "Let's go," I replied, "I don't feel like going to the toilet this afternoon." Ribka simply remained seated. The guard gave us a long look and then left the door open. Maybe he thought Ribka had found her prey.

"Abeba."

"Yes, Ribka."

"Be careful about that idiot Tsegga," Ribka said angrily. I must have shown my surprise. "I'm sorry, but she always makes me so mad. I can't stand her any more. The fool trusted an *afagn*."

"Excuse me, but is Tsegga not your friend? Are you not charged together?" I asked.

Ribka didn't answer, but sighed. "I'm warning you," she said, "be careful what you say to her."

Then she continued: "That night. Oh yes, that night at the Expo...." Ribka had a faraway look.

I was curious, and I was getting impatient. "Which night? What happened?"

Her eyes were red. There were no tears but her lips were quivering and her face became contorted. She told me quickly, as though she had but a few minutes to live and had to get the information out.

Being young, Ribka and Tsegga had been fairly open about their activities as underground members of the ELF. Both were in the tenth grade and they had been captured as they were leaving school.

Ribka came from a well-to-do family. Tsegga lived with an aunt while her mother was in Rome working as a housemaid. Tsegga was an illegitimate child and her father had never shown much interest in her.

Ribka had dark complexion, a high forehead, a straight nose, and compelling eyes. Tsegga was light-skinned, tall, and slightly plump; she had lovely eyelashes and beautiful teeth. I believe the *afagn's* main interest in them, was as beautiful young girls and only secondarily as members of the front.

After the *afagn* forced the two girls into their car, they didn't drive them to one of the prisons, but instead went straight to the old naval station and locked them in an office. The station was once the navy annex of the Kagnew Communication Station, which employed and housed some five thousand American service personnel. The buildings, including a modern school and hospital, were taken over by the Dergue's armed forces when the U.S. staff and their families were evacuated in 1974.

Ribka and Tsegga were locked away from half past four in the afternoon until half past ten that night. Then the two *afagn* returned, dressed up and perfumed, and apologized for being so late in bringing them something to eat. The girls were puzzled. One of the men took Ribka's hand and the other took Tsegga's, and they led them out to separate cars. As long as they were together, the girls had not been too concerned. But the moment they were denied the chance to say goodbye to each other, Ribka and Tsegga were gripped by fear.

To make matters worse, their hands were cuffed as soon as they got in the cars.

"I hate to do this to you, my angel, but it's only for your own protection," the *afagn* said to Ribka as he started the car.

My angel? For my own protection? She was confused. Ribka saw the trap when the *afagn* pulled up to one of the living quarters of the naval compound after a drive of a few minutes. One room seemed to have been prepared for a romantic evening: slow Amharic music, dim lighting, two cushioned chairs in front of a large mirror, and a bed.

"My duty and my commitment to the revolution have forced me to capture you. But you are so beautiful. Oh, God, why don't you tell me everything, and then I might even save you by marrying you?"

The *afagn* sat close to Ribka and removed her handcuffs. He did not bother to wait for an answer, but moved even closer and began to stroke her hair.

"His hands felt like snakes and his breath was like fire," Ribka recalled. She tried everything to avoid being raped. "Leave me alone. Either take me to prison or kill me," she shouted, pulling away from his grip.

"I won't hurt you. I love you, Ribka. Please understand," he said as he started unbuttoning his pants.

Ribka reached for his revolver on the bedside table — even though she had no idea how to use it. Before she had a chance to try her skills, however, her abductor twisted her hand and snatched the gun away from her.

She screamed at the top of her lungs, and when she saw that this upset him she kept it up. She began fighting back with her fists. She ripped his shirt with her teeth. The afagn was astonished; it had never occurred to him that he would meet with such resistance. His elaborate plan had failed.

He cuffed Ribka's hands again and straightened his

clothes hastily, slapped her hard on the face several times, and dragged her back to the car. He drove in the direction of the Expo Prison but then pulled into an empty lot and pointed his revolver at Ribka's chest. "If you're saving your virginity for a rebel, you won't live that long. I'm going to finish you off right now."

Ribka screamed even louder and longer than she had before — louder and longer than she thought it possible for a person to scream. But it paid off; the *afagn* became frightened and put the gun away. It was a miracle, Ribka felt, that he didn't shoot her then and there and dump her body somewhere. At half past one in the morning they reached the Expo Prison. He removed the cuffs once again and handed her over to the prison authorities. Then he left.

Ribka was held for two days in a room by herself without food or water, and without anybody so much as checking on her. Her body was a mass of bruises. Wherever the *afagn's* hand had touched her intimately, particularly her breasts and her thighs, she furiously cleaned herself with her own saliva, remembering her ordeal with a sense of revulsion.

As she told me the story I boiled inside. "So that was the night... What a night!"

"— No... that wasn't it..." Ribka answered, and continued with the rest of her story.

In the one month that she was kept at the Expo Prison, Ribka underwent rigorous interrogation. She was immersed in a barrel of cold water that contained the vomit and blood of previous victims. She was subjected to electric shock. Her abdomen was stomped upon. She was forced into the number eight position, just as Semhar had been, and the soles of her feet beaten. But the worst torture, said Ribka, was number nine.

"My big toes were tied together and my hands were tied together, and I was made to lie on my stomach. Then they pulled my toes over my back as far as they would go and beat me over the feet. They're such madmen. I thought my whole body was going to come apart then and there."

Ribka was kept in solitary confinement so that, unlike Fana, she had nobody to tend her wounds. Her parents inquired from prison to prison, checked the morgue, and tried to find out if she had joined the fronts. But they discovered nothing. As a result there were no food parcels for Ribka; once a day she was given leftovers from the other prisoners or from the guards.

The guards gave her one ill-fitting dress, and oddly enough it looked familiar to Ribka; in fact, it was exactly like Tsegga's dress. They also gave her a blanket, three days after her arrival, and a bar of soap. She was only permitted to wash herself once a week in a small mud-floored room. Bugs and lice became her constant companions.

Expo had been built as a landmark industrial and economic development project. The huge compound near Asmara airport contained several fanciful pavilions and the grounds were set off with beds of colorful flowers. The unveiling of the exhibition had been much heralded, and when it opened in 1969 it attracted throngs of local residents and tourists alike.

Then, at the height of the wave of indiscriminate arrests in Asmara, in March 1975, this symbol of economic prosperity and faith in the future was converted to a military camp and prison. No modifications were made to the buildings themselves. Some rooms at the Expo Prison contained anywhere from one to a hundred prisoners.

Ribka was alone in a fairly large room that had a window. The sky and the trees that she saw through the window, and when she was taken outdoors for a moment by the guard, became her only solace. She made an attempt to talk to the young guard who accompanied her outside, but he remained stony and silent.

Ribka denied all the charges leveled against her, primarily being an ELF underground cell leader with a network of contacts throughout the city; and she refused to incriminate anyone else.

"That night" — the night that continued to haunt and torment Ribka, the night that she had been so anxious to tell me about — actually began early one morning when a guard brought her fresh-smelling soap and a towel and then escorted her to a room that had a shower. She happily washed her broken body, even taking advantage of the extra water to wash her filthy clothes.

Ribka found her room swept when she returned. Not only that, but an army nurse dressed her wounds and she was given a good meal and a hot cup of tea! The interrogation is over, she thought, maybe I'll soon be out of here. She visualized herself standing tall among her comrades, having endured so much pain and suffering in the service of her motherland.

The day's special treatment naturally revived Ribka. She sat on the folded blanket and braided her hair, wishing she had a mirror. She thought of her boyfriend and she checked her breast, which was still healing from a cigarette burn, where one of her interrogators had extinguished his cigarette. She dismissed the idea of ever having a baby; she did not want to remember the morning her abdomen was stomped upon and the agonizing pain that followed.

After the refreshing shower and the food, she wanted to live, love, and work for the cause. With these wonderful ideas, though, came the thought of her friend Tsegga. Where could she be? Why did they not put us together? Could she be dead? How do they know what we did together — even day by day? Who could have given them the names of the three people the interrogators had mentioned? Nobody knew them but Tsegga and me.

There were no answers. Ribka preferred to daydream about her future. That day, she was given a second meal. Soon after, a guard opened the door to her room and was unusually pleasant. He helped her up and enquired about her feet before leading her outside. This kind treatment boosted Ribka's morale. After a short walk, they arrived at a room so large that it must have been a showroom for machinery back in the Expo days, but now flimsy boards had been used to partition it into offices.

A Major in a smart uniform walked through the door and quickly sat down. He gestured for Ribka to take a seat as well. The guard left them.

"If we had no evidence, we would have released you by now," said the Major, resting his hand on the untidy desk and fiddling with a pencil. "But the odds are against you, beautiful Ribka. We're giving you one more chance to confess. I don't know what kind of spell your *shifta (bandit)* men have you under."

Prisoner and interrogator faced each other sternly. The Major waited for Ribka's response. But her lips were sealed tighter than ever.

"This is the end for you, rebel. Goodbye," said the Major, leaving the room.

Two guards entered immediately and took Ribka to a two-room building. One of them pushed her into the exceptionally small toilet, which could barely hold the three of them standing up. The other guard chained her hands and feet. Ordering her to call "guard" when she was ready to confess, they closed the door behind them.

Ribka was left in total darkness. The smell was so bad that she could not help but vomit. While trying to lift her hand out of the chains to wipe her mouth, she fell face down and hit her head, and she could not get up. The chains were so tight that she felt the veins in her hands and feet popping. Her whole body hurt.

Hours passed, Ribka said; "But I had no intention of confessing anything to those *deki kelbi* [sons of bitches]."

She could hear the guard outside the door as he paced back and forth; he was expecting her call. That guard left and after a few minutes she heard the footsteps of two others.

Soon the toilet door was opened and the light was switched on. Ribka saw the blood from her head drip down over her face into the toilet. One of the guards picked her up and asked if she was ready to confess. There was no reply from Ribka. Then they departed, leaving the toilet door open.

Minutes later, the *afagn* who had taken Tsegga from the naval office came in holding hands with a well-dressed, well-coiffed woman wearing large sunglasses. Both of them made an effort to stand in the doorway of the toilet, but they found the stench unbearable. Ribka's heart started beating furiously. She was shaken at the idea of who the woman might be.

It can't be her, she thought. No... it couldn't be, hand in hand with the very *afagn* who arrested us. Surely she must be suffering like me, either here or in some other prison — or else she's dead. Maybe I've lost too much blood and am not seeing right.

The woman slowly removed her sunglasses and their eyes met. What Ribka had feared and suspected in the deepest recesses of her heart had come true, and the reality was ugly indeed. It was Tsegga. Of all the physical and psychological torture Ribka had undergone at the hands of the thugs, this was the very worst.

Ribka kept shaking her head in disbelief even as she told me the story. Tsegga sobbed as they faced each other, but Ribka had no reason to cry; after all, she had acted heroically and was at peace with herself. His mission accomplished, the *afagn* tried to console Tsegga, then took her away. It was a long time before Ribka would come to terms with the truth. That was the night Ribka was talking about.

The pain from the cuts on her forehead and her swollen wrists and ankles worsened; the smell of the toilet became more and more unbearable. Towards dawn, Ribka found that she could not continue in such agony. The heroic girl was only human, after all, with human limitations. She gave testimony that the three businessmen that Tsegga had incriminated had fully cooperated with them. She also gave the names of her underground cellmates. Ribka had a wider circle of contacts than Tsegga did, and she would not betray those contacts whom Tsegga did not know; but she confirmed the information that Tsegga had already spilled.

If a prisoner withstands all the cruel methods of interrogation, both physical and psychological, and still refuses to give in, word leaks out, and the prisoner is considered a hero. But if you surrender, and especially if you betray someone — no matter how unbearable the torture — you are treated like a leper. It is better to die defiant and victorious in the dungeons.

"Of all the countless times that my interrogators pointed their revolvers at my temple, how I wish one of them had pulled the trigger," Ribka told me. "Everything would be over now. I would have passed into history as a heroine. Why was I spared? Why didn't the ground of the Expo, softened by the sweat and blood of so many prisoners, simply swallow me up? Or why didn't I pass into oblivion when the gangsters threw me into the toilet and I fell on my head? You have no idea how I feel when I see the contemptuous looks of the other prisoners at toilet time. I didn't confess everything, just the version Tsegga had already admitted to; and anyway, I'll deny everything in court — if I'm lucky enough to stand trial, that is.

"Do you believe me?" Ribka asked at the end of her painful story.

How could I help but feel compassion for her? I was so choked up with tears that I could not speak. I drew her near and hugged her. With our hands clasped and our tears mingling the idea of prayer came to both of us at the same time and we prayed silently. We felt one and the same. At that particular moment, the cell looked spacious and illuminated; the silence and peace was overwhelming.

I assured Ribka that it was not irresponsibility, careless-ness, or malice that had made her break down, and that she was still a heroine.

Three days after the incident in the toilet, Tsegga joined Ribka in prison, no longer looking glamorous but dressed plain-ly, her hair dishevelled.

I asked Ribka if she had now forgiven both herself and Tsegga. As she replied, "yes," her eyes brightened, and a smile gradually took over her pale, half-dead face — it was the kind of smile that I had never seen in my life before and have never seen again to this very day.

"One more thing," she said, all her rage and anxiety hav-ing vanished. "Let me tell you this before the others come back. They're still trying to use us. They told Tsegga and me to spy on you. You know I won't.

Ribka was exhausted from reliving her ordeal, but she felt a great sense of relief. Our cellmates returned to find her resting her head on a folded blanket with me caressing her forehead. Fana and Tsegga were both disturbed when they saw us, but for entire-ly different reasons: Fana was afraid for me, while Tsegga was afraid for herself, worried that Ribka had told me her story.

Although the other women in the cell had known about the Expo Prison, it was Ribka who woke us up to the true horrors of this infamous hellhole. She had been directly and indirectly exposed to the atrocities. Young boys terrified at the mere sight of armed soldiers were beaten to death, their innocent cries chilling the souls of the other prisoners. Some were made to get up at five in the morning and to dig for hours under the scorching sun, with-out food or water, only to be shot in the back of the head, their bodies slumping into the graves they had spent the whole day dig-ging.

Prisoners who could not tolerate the horror would often lose their minds before they were shot. The head of the Expo Prison, the notorious Colonel Zenebe Asfaw, a beast in human form, was well known for detaining businessmen on false charges and releasing them after receiving thousands of dollars in bribes. He was also famous for torturing his prisoners personally, inflict-ing pain until rivers of sweat would run down his own brutal face.

The number of prisoners killed at the Expo Prison, either during interrogation or at random, is staggering. Many were maimed and disfigured. The wonderful Expo had become the Auschwitz of Africa.

Tsegga did not have Ribka's intuition, intelligence, or sense of duty — and growing up with her aunt, who brewed and sold *mies*, did not help. But my heart went out to the poor girl. She was just another victim of the times. On her third day at the Expo prison, the *afagn* had told her that Ribka had already confessed and that she was fighting a losing battle. He convinced her that the only way she could escape imprisonment was by marrying him, and that they would move to Addis Ababa. She would accept, she decided, and then find a way to join her mother in Italy.

Tsegga had been at the Expo Prison the whole time that Ribka was undergoing her torture. She had been given a decent room with a private bathroom, and she received food and clothing from her aunt. The familiar but ill-fitting dress that had been passed along to Ribka was in fact Tsegga's.

She and her *afagn* made a few trips to the city at night so that she could point out the homes of the members of her underground group; all but one, fortunately, had disappeared the afternoon that she and Ribka had been arrested.

Lanky, quiet Saba, who even had lanky hair, was about Fana's age, although she looked much older. Her face revealed the hard road she had traveled. Saba was born to poor farming parents in a village near Asmara. With no dowry and not having been bestowed with natural beauty, her chances of marrying were slim. She was declared a spinster at the age of nineteen, meaning she could be considered for marriage only by a divorced man, whether or not he had children. This was humiliating; but poor Saba was not lucky enough even to find a divorced man.

Saba's life was limited to keeping house and helping her father with his small farm. She resented the fact that she was not able to give her parents the joy of seeing her married. The parents, in turn, felt guilty because they had no dowry to offer a prospective husband. Her mother spent hours in church praying that Saba would someday get married. They did finally have one daughter who found a husband, but it was not Saba, it was her younger sister with fine features and beautiful long hair.

One day, Saba went with her father to *Bahri* for the harvest. The EPLF were very active in the area at that time. Their priority was to train the local residents to defend themselves against the enemy, and their second objective was to eradicate illiteracy. Saba decided to stay behind in Bahri and participate in the EPLF program. A whole world was opened to her there, not only because she learned to read and write, but also because she came to own a small plot of land through an EPLF redistribution scheme.

Saba's life was transformed. She had found a purpose. It was by pure coincidence that she was arrested. There was not even a particular charge against her.

She had come to Asmara on an EPLF errand and had stayed overnight at the home of a distant relative who sold *sewa* for a living in the Abashawul section. Two villagers carrying sacks of grain on their donkeys went inside the *sewa* house for a flask of the drink, leaving their donkeys outside. When Ethiopian secret police saw the donkeys, they went inside and accused the villagers of bringing the sacks of grain for *tegadelti*. The protestations of the men that the grain was for their families fell on deaf ears, and the two as well as Saba and the owner of the *sewa* house were taken to the Palace Prison. The owner of the *sewa* business was let go the next day, and the two villagers were released after five days. Saba had been there seven days when I joined them. She was never interrogated. I don't believe they even suspected her of anything.

Saba was exceptionally tight-lipped. She listened to every word spoken in the cell as though she were in class, and she spoke only about her youngest brother. She was desperately afraid something would happen to him back in their village.

When my cellmates had prayed together for me during my first call for interrogation, I had been impressed by their solidarity. But I soon learned that the truth was otherwise.

Everybody in the prison, men and women, knew that Ribka and Tsegga had betrayed some people. Ribka hated Tsegga, although she did forgive her at least momentarily when she shared her tragic story with me. Semhar resented Ribka and Tsegga's comfortable upbringing, yet at the same time she felt superior to them because she had betrayed no one. Fana hated and mistrusted both Tsegga and Ribka, while Saba thought the lot of us were just spoiled city women. But every one of them believed in God, in the power of prayer, and in Eritrea!

In the depths of my heart, I felt an urgent need for us to clear the air, to bring new life to our cell, to reconcile our differences and become one in spirit. So I decided to bring up the matter the day after Ribka had told me about her experiences. I decided I would start the discussion after we had finished supper.

"Get ready for the toilet," a guard shouted, and I heard one door cell after the other being opened. I followed the footsteps and heard the prisoners whisper among themselves. Our door was opened and we were let out after the first half of the prison population had come back from their toilet visit.

I looked at the pale blue sky and the patches of soft white clouds. In the lonely or sad moments of my life, I had nearly always found strength in looking at the sky, just as in the happy moments of my life it had given me added joy.

We visited the toilet quickly, under guard as usual, meeting the five prisoners from the other women's cell as well as some of the men at the outdoor faucet. I wondered how life was in their cells — particularly the women's — thinking that the atmosphere could very well be just as tense as it was in our own. We all washed our hands and returned to our cell. Soon after we finished eating the leftovers from the various lunch parcels sent by our families, I had a feeling that the time was right.

I glanced at the women and cleared my throat to begin. At that moment there came a knock on the wall from the prisoners in the next cell. Time for evening prayer. It started with the traditional Coptic Orthodox prayer: "Forgive us, O Lord, for Christ's sake. In the name of the Holy Mother, Mary, forgive us." The names of all the saints were chanted. We ended with the Lord's Prayer.

"Well, time to lie down. Spread out the blankets," Tsegga said, starting to get up.

"I'd like to say something if we can stay up a little longer," I said.

I might as well get right to the point, I thought.

"We all pray together for our release and for peace," I

began. "But God will not answer our prayers if we keep on nursing resentment and hatred for one another."

But I had simply set off Fana's ire: "How can you trust traitors and sluts like these two?" She spat the words out, her finger darting in the direction of Ribka and Tsegga. "They gave in and cooperated with them — with the goddamn Amharas!"

Semhar shrugged and nodded her agreement with Fana.

Stubborn Ribka reacted violently to Fana's accusation, and she lashed back, "Mind your own business. Who are you to judge us, to call us sluts? Of all the nerve — a bar woman like you! If there's any whore here, it's you," she roared.

No one spoke for a moment, but by the flickering light from the candle smuggled into our cell I saw that Saba's teeth were clenched. "How could those two fools give in to the Amharas?" she muttered.

I had not expected this dismal scene. It was not only embarrassing, but frightening. Oh God, I thought, this could come to blows! What have I started?...

"Shhh, shhh, please..." I pleaded. "We can't afford to argue like this. The guards will be here. Look at how self-righteous we all are!"

Then, for reasons that I cannot understand, our cell slowly became enveloped in almost total silence. I had planned to deliver a little lecture on forgiveness and self-restraint, but in the dead silence that had somehow been created, the idea of telling them the story of Irène Laure, a member of the French Resistance during the German occupation of France, came to mind.

"Throughout history, people from various nations have been either oppressed by their own people in the name of government authority or enslaved by foreign aggressors," I began. There was still the odd venomous glance being exchanged among the women, but I forged ahead. "People have worked hard, suffered greatly, been imprisoned, impoverished, and even killed in order to attain their freedom, as we Eritreans are doing now. Let me tell you about Madame Irène Laure, a woman who I admire, and who I met in 1969 during the Moral Re-Armament conference in Asmara."

Tsegga and Ribka seemed to have heard of Moral Re-Armament and the conference I was mentioning. I could tell from the expressions on the faces of the others that they had not, but they were all showing signs of surrendering to the story. The delicate orange and yellow glow of the little candle on the floor was beautiful. The silence was enormous. My mind was clear.

"Irène Laure was born in France in 1898. Her well-to-do parents took great pains to shelter her from the misery of the world, but little Irène refused to close her eyes. Her father had a construction business and, at a tender age she wondered why her father's workers had only plain bread and onions for lunch, and why they had no socks or decent winter boots. But she never got a satisfactory answer to her questions. She stole cakes and chocolates and gave them out to the men until she was caught red-handed. As far as she was concerned she was only doing what was fair and natural.

"At the age of fifteen Irène organized the distribution of milk to illegitimate children, and she gave her pocket money away to their mothers. When she was sixteen she joined the socialist party, against the wishes of her parents. She thought that class war would solve the problems of the French workers and the poor helpless mothers.

"When war was declared in Europe in 1914, Irène went to work in a hospital. For four years she tended the wounded and shared their suffering. She came out at the end of the war with a nursing diploma, more determined than ever to fight poverty and injustice.

"Irène married and already had five children when the Second World War broke out. When her eldest son dashed into the kitchen and told her that the Germans were already in Paris, she vowed to herself that she would never surrender. She decided to join the Resistance movement, and her husband and children — even the youngest ones — rallied behind her. She narrowly escaped death many times, as head of a medical team. But she was a woman of courage. The sight of little French children, even her own two youngest, slowly turning into little skeletons; the imprisonment and torture of her eldest son; the tortured bodies of her friends in the Resistance, who were even denied decent burials, all served to make Irène even more daring, more committed, and more bitter in her hatred of the Germans. Toward the end of the war, when American bombers filled the French skies, Irène wished to see every German city destroyed. She rejoiced at the thought of Germany in ruin.

"After the War, the indomitable Irène went on to help and found no less than seventeen organizations for the homeless, the orphaned, the people from concentration camps. On top of all this, she was elected to the French parliament as a representative of the Socialist Party. She worked day and night toward the realization of a peaceful and prosperous France. As a diehard socialist, she also wanted to see a united and peaceful Europe.

"In the summer of 1947, Irène Laure was invited to attend a Moral Re-Armament conference in Caux, Switzerland. On the day of her arrival, while walking from her room to the conference hall, she spotted German delegates, and she went straight back to her room and packed to leave. Just as she got to the door, though, she ran into Dr. Frank Buchman, the founder of Moral Re-Armament. When she told him she could not stay under the same roof with Germans, he said: 'Madame Laure, you are a socialist, and you want to see a united and prosperous Europe. How can you expect to rebuild Europe if you reject the German people?' His words went through her like a knife. She wrestled bitterly with her feelings throughout the night, remembering all the suffering and death that the Germans had inflicted upon her people. She could not shake off the memory of her two children waking in the night and drinking water to quell their hunger. She thought of her friends in the Resistance who were with her one hour only to be liquidated the next. Dr. Buchman had created a terrible dilemma for her, but toward dawn she finally decided to stay at the conference and let go of her hatred. In the depths of her heart, she knew that Germany could not be excluded from the map of Europe and that a united Europe could be built only on forgiveness and love."

When I had finished telling Irène Laure's story, I said: "My dears, it would be a disservice to our heroic *tegadelti* who fall in battle, to the mothers who suffer in silence the loss of their husbands and children, to our children who die potbellied due to malnutrition, to our pregnant women whose stomachs were slit with a sword and their stillborns tossed in the air, to our men who go off to work and never make it home, to the children whose limbs are hacked off by the enemy, to all those whose lives are a constant nightmare — it would be a disservice to all — if we did not for-give and love one another."

I told them that just as Irène Laure could not hope to see a united and peaceful Europe without Germany, we could not say we love our country and then refuse to understand and forgive our fellow Eritreans.

"Look at the price we are paying. Ribka and Tsegga have suffered so much. Let us not judge. Let us search our hearts." Tears were running down my cheeks.

Tsegga began to sob, and her burst of emotion quickly spread through the tiny cell. She told us that she never would have given in if they had not tricked her into believing that Ribka had already confessed. The moment that she stood face to face with Ribka by the stinking toilet came back to her in nightmares. She fell to her knees and asked Ribka's forgiveness. Ribka simply cried her heart out.

Fana apologized for her self-righteousness with tears streaming down her face.

Semhar's resentment appeared to vanish into thin air.

Saba told how she had felt worthless when her sister, who was four years her junior, got married, and how she had bitterly hated the world. True, she had found a new life with the EPLF, but it was taking time for her wounds to heal.

Our cell was transformed. The prayer we said that night before we slept is as vivid in my mind as though it were only yes-terday.

I was too excited to sleep. In my half-awake state, my mind wandered and raced: I saw the Ethiopian soldiers and the *afagn* with all their wickedness leaving Eritrea and our *tegadelti* proud-ly marching into the capital; I saw the blue Eritrean flag glorious-ly flying on all the government buildings and I heard the church bells ringing out with joy; I saw fathers and mothers embracing their *tegadelti* sons and daughters; I saw myself embracing my brothers and sisters who were away from home — my sisters Demekesh and Medhin and my brothers Petros, Paulos, and Solomon.

Then I saw the Eritrean flag flying at half-mast for those who had lost their lives in order to bring dignity and justice to their homeland. I saw myself working with my Eritrean sisters to rebuild the beleaguered little nation whose people have suffered so much for so long.

I was overwhelmed. I could not shake from my mind the sights and sounds of a free and prosperous Eritrea, yet stark reality stared me in the face. Were my brothers Dawit and Michael held under lock and key also? I wondered. Were they being tortured and tormented at that very moment?

I saw my own four children standing at the front gate waiting forlornly for their mother to come home.

# Five

    The Ethiopian military government used various methods of arrest. They took people from their hospital beds. They nabbed newlyweds at the bus station or at the airport as they returned from their honeymoon and sent them to different prisons. They took workers from their offices, assuring them that they wanted only to talk to them for a few minutes, as they did with me. They took people aside in factory corridors as they were leaving work for the day and told them they were under arrest. They snatched people out of their beds in the middle of the night, without giving them time to put on their pants the half-asleep, confused victims would leave their family behind helpless and devastated.

    The experience can haunt a victim for years and years.

    Soldiers would surround the house and then break through the door as though they expected to be met by hundreds of armed resisters. They might show up at a school and talk politely and amicably, and then with lightning speed shove the victim into their car, as they did with Ribka and Tsegga. When they burst into a home, they would go on a rampage in search of evidence, emptying wardrobes onto the floor, sweeping books and precious objects from shelves, dumping out bags, throwing the contents of desks to the floor. If they found anything of value, they would simply take it. The soldiers of the Dergue had a special craving for radios, wristwatches, gold, and, of course, cash.

    Just as there were various ways of arresting people, there were also many techniques, both psychological and physical, for torturing the victim:

    **Foul language:** This can have a powerful effect on a person from a religious background or someone who has been brought up in a refined or sheltered environment.

**Sudden reversal of tone:** First, the interrogator will be pleasant and friendly, courteously addressing you by name. Then all of a sudden his mouth will twitch, his eyebrows will knit together, and he will shout, "You idiot, I will blow your brains out!" Then he will come at you with outstretched fingers as though he is about to pluck your eyes out.

**Night interrogation:** This method was used only rarely while I was in prison, and its employment depended on the gravity of the alleged offence. Jolted from sleep in the middle of the night, the victim is in a confused and drowsy state of mind, and is therefore far more vulnerable than usual.

**Intimidation of all sorts, often accompanied by lies:** "If you confess," they might say, "especially if you tell us who your contacts are, we will let you go. Did you not hear that so and so was freed a week ago after she signed a confession?" (When in fact the prisoner in question has only been transferred to another prison, or the interrogator may have simply invented a name.) Or they will say, "If you confess you will not be interrogated any more. We will send you to Sembel Prison for a month or so to be rehabilitated and then you will be free." Or "If you continue with this stubbornness, denying what we already know about you, we will finish you off." There is no limit to the lies the prison lords are capable of telling. They will do anything and everything to induce a prisoner to confess.

**Use of loved ones:** This is the most effective method of all. They might say, for instance, "Your brother has already been arrested, but his fate depends on you. He is being questioned in the next room." And through the wall you can actually hear someone screaming and wailing.

**Suspense:** They might not call you for interrogation for days on end. You are left to imagine the very worst.

There is a wide array of ways in which bodily harm is inflicted for the purpose of extracting information from prisoners.

**Beating:** This could be all over the body, but the soles of the feet are the favorite spot. The torturer may stand on the prisoner's back and beat the soles violently with a rubber truncheon; then the victim is made to walk on gravel, pressing the feet down as hard as possible until blood spurts.

**Immersion in water:** The head is dunked into a barrel of

icy cold water until the victim chokes; the blood and vomit of other inmates most often floats on the surface of the water.

**Electric shock.**

**Burning:** A cigarette is ground out on the flesh of the victim.

**Kicking** women in the abdomen, resulting in injury to the uterus; methodically **squeezing** the genitals of male prisoners; There is no comparison to the pain of these two torture techniques; the victim usually falls unconscious.

Physical torture invariably brings on a heavy menstrual flow, and the women are not given sanitary napkins nor are they permitted to wash themselves.

Interrogation and torture are not carried out by a few miscreants who happen to have lost their souls, but by dozens of specially-trained human animals who have absolute authority over their defenceless victims. How a mortal can inflict such cruelty on his fellow human beings is a mystery to me. After all I have gone through and seen, I still do not want to acknowledge the existence of such evil.

In my own case, after the sudden change of tone and dismissal, with my interrogators telling me that they were giving me one more night to think things over, seven days elapsed without a word. Although by then I had developed strong bonds with my cellmates, not knowing my fate left me very uneasy, to say the least. Moreover, the sight of men mercilessly beaten and left in the corridor to crawl like babies to their cells; of priests dragged by their mantles and beards; of women humiliated by the interrogators' vulgar language; plus the wailing and groaning of freshly beaten prisoners, and Ribka's Expo stories were painful to me, the random sound of gunshots — in short, the prison atmosphere, the holocaust of our time and place — was all too much for me to bear, I fell ill.

During the months preceding my imprisonment, I had lost a great deal of weight — more than was good for my already thin body. Now I had no resistance left at all. My chronic gastritis turned acute and with it came terrible headaches. The fifth day after my arrival in prison I vomited ceaselessly. I then became very weak and completely lost my appetite.

On about my eighth day in prison, I was called again for

interrogation. Since I was unsteady on my feet, two guards helped me climb the stairs to the interrogation room. The interrogators had written the charges themselves and they motioned for me to sign. I simply stared at them. I had no intention of falling into their trap nor had I the energy to speak. They most likely thought my days were numbered, but our worries were quite different. The interrogators were afraid that I would not hang on long enough to give them the information they were looking for; and I was afraid that I would not last to tell the world about their crimes. They called two of my cellmates to come and take me back to the cramped cell.

Another week passed, and my health only worsened. Then I was called again. I had to labor hard to climb the stairs, gasping for breath with every step as I was helped along by a guard.

This time, my two assigned interrogators had been joined by the head of the Palace Prison, the Major, and the director of all the prisons in Asmara, the Colonel. I was told to sit on a chair facing all four interrogators. The atmosphere was tense. It was not easy to confront these men who had the power to decide at the drop of a hat whether their victim lived or died.

There was an awesome silence of some ten minutes. Then the Colonel began, looking right into my eyes: "Woman, speak the truth, and we will spare you from death by sickness here... or...."

He glanced at the revolver that sat on the table within his reach. All eight eyes were staring at me, but somehow I was not intimidated. I was there in body but not in spirit; I was looking at my interrogators but I did not see them. I was so engrossed in my own world that I remembered I was under interrogation only when the Colonel called me names at the top of his voice. Miraculously, he cooled off a little, but then resumed questioning. I remained calm, although the hard chair was becoming unbearable.

"You collected seven thousand dollars for the rebels from two businessmen, and you gave it to your brother Petros who left Asmara in March to join them. The day before his departure, you had dinner together and talked about how you would raise more money and give it to him at a certain time and place. Do you deny this?"

"It never happened."

"At some point in April, did he not telephone and ask you to pick up money from one of his contacts?"

I felt an electric shock jolt through my body.

"Petros *is* your brother, is he not, you stubborn fool?" the Major roared.

"Yes, he is my brother."

"What is wrong with helping a brother who happens to be an EPLF agent? Helping the rebels amounts to helping him, does it not?"

"My brother never needed any help from me."

"Speak up, woman. Tell the truth before I wring your neck," boomed one of my regular interrogators.

But now the Colonel was very calm. "You were not limited to collecting money from business people and sending it to the so-called freedom fighters," he asserted. "As head of the Relief and Rehabilitation Association for Eritrea, you were indirectly sending food and supplies to the rebels. Is that not so?"

It struck me that they looked and sounded like actors on a stage, furious and out of control one minute, cool and collected the next. I summoned what little energy I could and spoke:

"That association was not a one-woman show. It was a formal organization with a board, staff, and auditors, and the government was following its activities very closely. True, the treasurer and I were signing checks for large amounts of money, but we never handled cash. Moreover, when the government took over, the books were very carefully audited and there was never any discrepancy. A discrepancy would never have been tolerated."

"Petros arranged for you to meet one of the rebel leaders in Barentu in October of 1974, and you kept the appointment. What do you say to this?"

"It is true that I went to Barentu in October, but for a different reason."

"What reason?"

"Our relief branch in Barentu had started an interesting rehabilitation programme and I went to see how it was progressing."

"You are lying, woman, you are lying," all of them seemed

to shout at once.

"Why are we listening to her when there is no question she is a traitor?" roared the Colonel. "We have to take action on this woman."

"This rebel deserves a bullet," muttered one of my two regular interrogators bitterly, clenching his teeth.

The next thing I knew I was back in my cell with two blankets folded under my head for a pillow. I learned that I had fainted from exhaustion and that they had called Semhar and Ribka to take me back to my cell.

After I had regained consciousness, my mind was clear and I had a sense of inner peace, helped along by soup sent from home.

The following day two guards escorted me back for another bout with the same four interrogators, and the same hard chair was waiting for me. I felt sure an extra fifty steps had been added to the stairs, I was so frail and spent.

"Woman," the Colonel began, "we already have plenty of evidence to prosecute you, despite your denials. Now we have additional tangible evidence, evidence that will be completely impossible for you to deny."

He cleared his throat and took on a more authoritative air.

"Your brother Petros and his friends have been captured in battle; no one can escape our sword! They are now in Kagnew Prison. He has confessed everything. You better give us your version before we bring him over here to challenge you. Once he tells the truth right to your face, there will be no clemency for you. We have been unusually considerate in your case. Think it over quickly — you have very little time."

This was the heaviest blow yet. I was shocked. Petros captured in battle? When? How? And they say he confessed! My mind drifted back to the days of our childhood.

I remembered being about six years old and Petros four. We were jumping on our beds when my dress caught on a pot of tea on the nightstand and it spilled over me. I was burned from my hips down. Petros cried out for help: "*Addei, Addei.*" Mother rushed to the scene and she and my grandmother carried me to the clinic in Acria. Although he had been told to stay behind, Petros insisted on following us; and when I cried as I was being treated by the nurse, I saw that his eyes were filled with tears.

"Speak up, woman!" yelled the Major.

My head was spinning. It got so heavy that my neck could hardly support it. Then a wonderful thing happened: a long-distance telephone call came through for the Major, and they immediately dismissed me in order to hold a conference among themselves.

The next morning at eleven o'clock I was called again. As I shuffled along to the interrogation room, my guard said: "I think your brother is here. You better confess before he testifies."

In my devastation I could not help but slow my pace, but I tried to act as though I had not heard what he had said. I only hoped it was a cruel lie.

In the interrogation room there were two new men, besides the Major and my usual interrogators. One of them kept leaving the room as though waiting for someone to arrive.

The Major was pacing and the atmosphere was tense and ugly.

Could what the guard had said on the way be true? I wondered. Is Petros really here?

After pacing up and down and searching the room with his eyes, the Major looked at my other interrogator and shouted: "Where are the prisoners?" Then his eyes turned to me and he said, "Close your eyes, rebel!"

Oh Lord, who am I going to see when I open my eyes?

My heart began pounding and my head was hurting.

"One last chance before your brother comes. Will you confess now?"

"I have no confession to make."

"Open your eyes, woman," the Major bawled.

Two prisoners stood in the corner opposite me, but neither of them looked anything like my brother Petros. I took a long, deep breath.

One of the two was a friend of my father, Ato Tesfai Woldemicael, a businessman whose large firm had been nationalized by the Dergue a few months previously. He had been arrested two days before me. I had never seen the other man before.

The interrogators and the Major brought in more chairs and sat down. They surveyed all three of us from head to toe. The

Major's tone changed completely. "Do you know this man, Abeba?" he said calmly, pointing to the stranger.

"No."

"Do you know this woman?" he asked the stranger.

"I have never met her, but I have heard about her commitment to the EPLF."

"Do you know this man?" the Major asked me, pointing to Ato Tesfai.

"Yes."

"Tell me about him." he continued.

"He is a regular customer of the airline. He used to charter small cargo planes."

"How much money did he give you to forward to the rebels through your brother Petros?"

"I know nothing about the man except that he is a customer of Ethiopian Airlines."

The other prisoner then testified that Ato Tesfai Woldmicael had told him personally that he had been contributing to the *tegadelti* through me.

But Ato Tesfai shouted, "Lies, pure lies! In fact, *this* man," and he pointed to the other prisoner, "came to my office and asked for money for the fighters, but I told him I did not want to help them or to have anything to do with them, and I threw him out of my office. I know this woman only through Ethiopian Airlines. I have never had anything else to do with her, nor have I had any contact with anybody connected with the fighters."

The interrogators were clearly disappointed. The Major got so furious that he dismissed me and kept the other two behind. They did not believe Ato Tesfai Woldmicael and he was later brutally beaten. But he never did give in; he never betrayed me.

Several days passed in limbo, and my strength did not return.

One morning we noticed that the guards were talking roughly and began to curse whenever a prisoner was called for interrogation. There was more tension than usual in the air the whole day. At five o'clock the guards rushed us for the afternoon toilet visit. I walked as quickly as I could, but at the end of the corridor I felt my knees buckling under: On the steps leading to the Major's office, right in front of me, was a man dressed in a white doctor's outfit — it was Dr. Assefaw Tekeste, chair of the Red Sea branch of our banned Relief and Rehabilitation Association for Eritrea.

My God! If they use with him the kind of trap they set for Tsegga, that will be it, I thought. Dr. Assefaw was implicated in a case that also concerned me indirectly. What if they tell him that I have already confessed? Will Dr. Assefaw know that one must always deny, deny, deny? But I was not called for interrogation the next morning, and I did not see Dr. Assefaw again at the Palace Prison. So many professionals were joining the front at that time that the Dergue had come up with the brilliant idea of transferring professionals such as medical doctors to Ethiopia without notice. I would later learn that Dr. Assefaw had been taken straight from his work at the Central Hospital in Massawa, kept one night at the *ghebi*, and immediately flown to Addis Ababa.

I had such a hideous night that the next day I developed a headache early in the morning, which grew worse with each passing hour. It felt like someone was banging on my head with a hammer. My eyes were stinging. My ears hurt. My tongue was dry. My stomach was burning. My whole body ached. It was unbearable; death would be a relief, I thought. My cellmates were asking me how I felt, but I was too weak and in too much pain to reply.

Semhar banged on the door and cried out for help. It may have been around three or four in the afternoon when a snarling guard came.

"What the hell is going on here, you idiotic rebels?" he fumed. "Who gave you permission to bang on the door like that?"

Ribka told him that I was fearfully sick, that he should report it to the head of the prison. The guard spitefully slammed the door with a bang that made my head hurt more than ever.

Then who should show up but the Major himself, threatening to punish my cellmates for their behavior. I heard him say: "She is such a fool. If only she had confessed by now she would be home with her children."

The Major left the door to the cell open and I could hear him grumbling as he stomped off down the corridor. The pain did not ease much throughout the night. In the morning, the Major came to check on me but I cannot remember what he said.

Toward the end of the third day after the terrible headache had begun, I perspired profusely; and as the beads of sweat ran from my forehead so did the migraine; the aches in my joints, the burning in my stomach, the pain throughout my whole body dwindled away, leaving me weaker than before but much more comfortable.

Three days later, at about ten in the morning, the door was opened slowly, unlike other days, and the guard asked me to come out. With my *netsela* (shawl) wrapped tightly around my waist to help me to walk straight, I followed him down the corridor and outside into the courtyard to a jeep that was parked near the office.

As we passed through the huge black iron gates of the Palace Prison, and saw Cinema Roma and the blue sky with its soft clouds and the people walking in the streets, I was euphoric. As we passed my parents' house, which was on the way to the army hospital, Selassamestegna, I grew nostalgic. I somehow expected to see my mother coming through the gate. Then I was gripped by fear. The horrors of the Expo Prison came to mind, and I imagined my brothers, Dawit and Michael, just twenty and eighteen years old, in the hands of the enemy. Oh God, please protect them, I implored. As we approached the gate of the hospital, I saw two lines of women and children, and others sitting on the lawn. The weather was perfect for lazily sitting about anywhere, but especially on beautiful grass with flowers scattered here and there. As I stepped out of the jeep and dragged myself slowly toward the entrance, I heard a murmur from the women sitting on the lawn: *"esregna... esregna"* — prisoner... prisoner.

One of my guards made his way inside. The other stood beside me in front of the door while the women in line fell away to let us pass. The doctor must have instructed us to wait. Leading me to a bench just inside the entrance, my guard gestured for me to sit. The driver and the other guard left us, saying they would check back before noon.

The women, Ethiopian armed forces wives, were staring at me, and I was marvelling at the brilliant reds, blues, yellows, and greens of their *shashes* — the scarves that Ethiopian women wind around their heads.

Half an hour passed with my young guard hovering over me. I decided to speak to him:

"You've been standing much too long. The rifle must be very heavy — why don't you sit here beside me and hold it in your lap?"

He looked at me wide-eyed.

"You can see that I'm too weak to even consider escaping," I continued. "Anyway, I have four daughters and all I want is to be legally free and to be with them."

"You are the mother of four children?"

"Yes, I am."

"How old are they?"

"The eldest is sixteen and the youngest five."

"And they are all girls? You mean you have no boys at all?"

"No, I don't. But I love my girls. I wouldn't trade anyone of them for anything."

The guard slowly removed the gun from his shoulder and sat on the bench with me. "I want to ask you something," he said. "Why do you want to sell your beautiful country to the Arabs? Asmara is the loveliest place I have ever been."

I just smiled wearily and asked him a question: "Where were you, and what did you do, before you came to Asmara?"

"I was in Debreberhan. In school. Seventh grade."

"Seventh grade!" I exclaimed. "The best time of my life was in school — particularly junior high."

"You went to school... and you were a seventh-grader once! This is so interesting."

He forgot for a moment that he was a uniformed guard and became his real self. I went on and told him what my favorite subjects were when I was in the seventh and eighth grade, how much I enjoyed school and all the fun that went with it.

The guard seemed fascinated. Then he sank into deep thought.

"You seem perturbed. Are you not feeling well?" I asked.

"No. No, I'm all right. I was just thinking about my mother, my poor mother."

"What about your mother?"

"Well.... It was a Saturday morning and we were standing near our neighbourhood playground in Debreberhan listening to a portable radio. A truck with soldiers stopped near us. The soldiers got out and forced us — my friends and I — to board the truck. We yelled and shouted, but it did no good. They also took two other groups of men and boys on the way. Finally, we arrived in Addis Ababa. After we had basic military training for three months, several of us were assigned to Eritrea. They told us how easy it would be to capture the bandits and take whatever we wanted from the people, but I knew it was a lie. I have not participated in any combat so far, but if I do I'll never make it — I've heard enough from the ones who have been there. I'm sure my mother thinks I'm dead by now. The people who saw us must have told her I was carted away to fight."

"And what about your father?" I asked.

"My father was in the military service and he died seven years ago. My mother raised my two younger sisters and me on her own."

My young guard tried to hide his face so that I would not see the tears welling up in his eyes.

"The situation we are all in now will come to an end." I said, "When you go back home, study hard — with an education you will be able to do whatever you want. If you become an educated, God-fearing, honest person, it will be a great tribute to your mother." I avoided his eyes for fear of embarrassing him.

I felt like hugging my guard and calling him "son," for he was only seventeen years old.

At that moment, I heard my name being called. I looked at my guard. Lifting his gun onto his shoulder again, he helped me up. I appreciated the support since I was already tired, and he held my arm until I had stepped into the doctor's office.

"*Selam*" — Hello, I said, bowing my head a little in a gesture of courtesy; but the short, dark-skinned doctor in his white gown had no intention of being friendly and merely motioned for me to sit. I suppose that just because I was outside the prison compound I had expected normal treatment! The guard went to the waiting room.

Sitting on a comfortable chair before a modest desk was a treat for me. I breathed deeply and tried to relax.

"What is your problem?" the doctor asked rudely.

What is my problem! This was not the approach I expected from a doctor.

"I am not feeling well."

I told him about my headaches and about the stomach ache that still persisted. I had lost my appetite and could not keep much down, I added, and I had a continual headache although it had become milder.

"How did this start?"

"I have dormant gastritis that flares up whenever I eat too much spicy food, but it has never been this bad. The constant headache is something new."

"When did all this happen?"

"Four days after my imprisonment."

"Exactly when?"

"The fourth of October."

He took my blood pressure and felt my pulse, handling me as though I were a piece of furniture. What happened to the oath that doctors and nurses take to treat every human being equally, friend and foe alike? I wondered. To put him at ease, I asked:

"Is my heart still beating? And how low is my blood pressure?"

The doctor tried to hide his smile. "You will survive, but I have to make blood and urine tests." He asked me all sorts of questions regarding my medical history. I had never had a serious problem, only appendicitis years earlier.

As I came out of the office my guard saw me and jumped up. "*Itiye* Abeba," he said. *Itiye* is a name given to an older sister in Amharic. "What did the doctor say, and what can I do for you?"

"I have to go to the other room for a specimen. You just make sure I don't escape," I joked.

He smiled a genuine, broad smile, and replied, "*Eshi*" — Okay.

As I sat on a bench in the corridor waiting for the test results, the doctor passed by and I asked if I could talk to him a moment. He nodded.

"Ever since I was arrested I have had no appetite," I said. "Now all of a sudden I feel hungry. I have no money with me, but I would be glad to give you some when I'm released. Could you please buy me something to eat?"

"We have a small cafeteria here but it is already closed. I

could bring you bread and tea. Would that help?"

"Of course. Anything would do."

Suddenly he said: "Woman, why did you get involved with those so-called freedom fighters? You should have just minded your own business and led a peaceful life."

When you do not know what to answer, it is best to keep quiet. I'm sure the doctor didn't expect a reply, at any rate, because he went on about his business. The hall was full of women with babies, many of them crying, and there were only two doctors and two nurses. When my doctor passed by again I reminded him, and after a while he returned with the bread, but no tea. I shared it with my new-found son.

The tests revealed that I had anaemia and an acute gastrointestinal disorder requiring bed rest and intravenous feeding. The doctor called the Major and told him that I should be hospitalized.

"We cannot afford a twenty-four-hour guard. Send her back here with her medication," said the voice at the other end.

"*Eshi, eshi*," – ok, ok– replied the doctor.

I could tell from the doctor's voice that the news was not good. He gave me various medications, including sleeping tablets, for I had told him I was not sleeping well. Just as I was about to leave, he made sure nobody was listening and said:

"Woman, your blood pressure is very low and your red cell count is way below normal. You are susceptible to any minor or serious disease. So be careful. Those damn rebels are the cause of all this. Unless they are totally wiped out Ethiopia will never have peace."

Our *tegadelti* are the cause of all this! What a joke, I thought. But all I said was, "Thank you, doctor."

As I turned to make my way to where Tadesse, my guard, was waiting — now joined by the other guard and the driver — I could tell by his face that the sweet, memorable mother-son relationship was over. We had become total foes again.

When I got back to the prison, the smiles and greetings of my cellmates seemed to be forced.

"When you were late, I hoped you had been admitted to hospital," said Ribka, stretching her legs as much as she could in the few feet of space we all had to share.

"It is better to be here with us than in the hospital with the Amharas," Saba cut in. "They could kill you with an injection." I was surprised by this comment, for Saba hardly ever said much.

Semhar, though sounding cool, expressed her happiness at my return.

Tsegga was continually glancing over at Fana, who was sitting in her usual position when she was in mental pain: knees drawn up under her chin, hands locked around her knees. She kept muttering over and over to herself: *"Ezen deki sheramuth meshemish tetzawitenalei"* — those rotten sons of whores, they finally got me.

Poor Fana had been called for interrogation.

When she had been thrown into prison, there was no specific charge against Fana; an Ethiopian army officer had simply done it for revenge after she had rejected his advances. The house of a new prisoner was normally searched immediately, but in Fana's case the search was carried out much later. To her husband's dismay, and to Fana's own surprise, an ELF newsletter was found in her bedroom. The handwriting of the scribbles in the margins was clearly hers; there was no way to deny it. When the interrogators presented Fana with the newsletter, she readily admitted to owning it. She knew that if she did not, her husband would be jailed as well. She said that she had accepted the newsletter under pressure from an ELF tegadelai who had threatened to shoot her. (A male fighter is a *tegadalai*; a female fighter a *tegadalit*.) Threatened or not, of course, she had been interested enough in the newsletter not to throw it out.

*"Deki sheramuth tetzawitenalei"* — the sons of whores, they got me, she kept repeating the whole evening. Fana's long-time dream of rearing the child she had had with a man she loved was crushed with the discovery of the newsletter.

As the days wore on, I noticed Fana becoming more and more revolutionary. I could envision her putting on trousers and taking up arms to fight the enemy.

There was nowhere for the prisoners to bathe at the Palace Prison. We would take the empty containers from our food parcels along with us on our afternoon toilet visit and fill them with water from the outdoor faucet; then we would wash ourselves in the stinking toilet. Since we had to do this on the run, we took turns — one day it would be Saba's turn, the next Tsegga's, so that all six of us usually got a chance once a week. One of us would hastily peel off an item of clothing and a couple of the others would hold the dress or the shirt and keep watch. Our families were allowed to send soap. We managed fairly well with a half gallon of water, but we had to be quick about it.

I had not taken advantage of the toilet visit since I had become ill, but the day after my trip to the hospital I had a sponge bath — *ghebi*-style — in the cell with a quart of water and Ribka's help.

Another five days passed in limbo, then it was back to the interrogation room. The medication had helped and I was eating better, but I was by no means strong. The walk up the stairs was laborious and there were no longer any hands to help — the guard now walked behind me.

My two interrogators were in their usual seats. How lucky I felt that my brother was not in their grip! If Petros had been captured, I reasoned, they would have brought him to the Palace Prison without delay.

"Sign this paper," ordered one of the men, rising from his chair and handing me his pen. I grabbed the pen. It was a good excuse to sit — I was already exhausted.

"What are you waiting for? Sign here," bellowed the younger, ruder of the two, pointing to the last line of two handwritten pages.

"Please let me read it first," I said politely.

"Do you think you are in your office? If you do not sign this paper immediately, we will arrest your husband, who is known to be your number one collaborator — and your father, too. As a matter of fact, it may interest you to know that we are also well aware of the fact that you have a rebel brother in America and that his name is Paulos. Our sword is long enough to reach him too. Never underestimate the revolutionary Ethiopian government. You don't want to spare yourself, which is hard to understand, but at least think of them."

This was just another of their ploys to make me admit to something, I figured, so I kept quiet. At this point, they looked at each other and left the room, leaving me alone. About fifteen minutes later they came back and saw that I had not signed the confession.

"Woman, we cannot go on giving you special treatment. We don't need to bring in your father or your husband. You have compelled us to take drastic action tomorrow. Guard, take this foolish rebel to her cell," ordered my younger interrogator.

The next day, an angry-looking guard dragged me from my cell and out into the compound where I saw three male prisoners facing a low wall, with four armed soldiers in front of them.

"Woman," a harsh voice called. "Line up with your comrades, hands behind your back, facing the wall."

While I slowly moved forward, I saw the soldiers aim their guns at us.

This is it, then, I thought. The end is here! There was no time to think of anything else. I just said a short prayer. Oh Lord, give me the courage to die bravely like so many of my people have, without screaming or begging for mercy, and receive me in Thy kingdom.

I closed my eyes as tightly as I could. Now and then I would hear the click of a gun, as though they were about to shoot. After about an hour I heard numbers being called — one... two... three.... And my mind went blank. Then I counted to a hundred myself... I was still alive!

I dared to slowly open my eyes. The four guns were still aimed at our foreheads. I closed my eyes.

The Major shouted, "For anybody willing to confess, I will count up to fifty." I counted to fifty with him.

"Fire," he screamed.

Seconds later my head was still on my shoulders! I glanced over at my brothers in death. They were alive too, with their hands behind their backs and their heads down, solemnly staring at the ground.

Suddenly I heard the singing of birds. I looked up. Not only were there dozens of birds victoriously flying about, but the sky was more beautiful than I had ever seen it. My inner voice said: be still and you will be okay. I had no watch but I could tell from the sun that about two hours had gone by.

Cold sweat started running down my face and my back and I was shaking like a leaf. Although my health had improved since I had started taking the medication, I was still weak and wobbly. Heaven knows how I managed to stand for so long.

At long last, the soldiers moved from their positions one by one. One of my interrogators ordered me to wait in the hallway. The other three prisoners were hurried back to their cells. I sat in the corridor for about half an hour; then came an order from the Major — solitary confinement.

The only two cells for women were already occupied, so solitary confinement was not possible. They therefore simply transferred me to a cell with four other women. Banishment to solitary confinement generally preceded the death penalty. The Major simply wanted me to be aware of their intentions. And the message was received.

When I was held in the Palace Prison there were very few female political prisoners in Asmara, although our numbers would increase dramatically over the years. There may have been a total of thirty when we were detained there. The women at the Palace Prison were either awaiting trial, waiting for transfer to Haz Haz Prison for Women, undergoing interrogation, or simply being held following interrogation. A few were released directly from the Palace.

My new cell was identical to the first; but there were five of us this time. One of my new cellmates happened to be Berekti, the aunt of my best friend from high school and a woman I liked very much. It was a lucky break; she made me forget about the ordeal of the afternoon and whatever fate was awaiting me the next day. I knew the other three young women from the toilet visits and our few stolen words en route, so we all hugged, talked a little, and prayed together. I talked almost through the night with Berekti.

She told me that when two *afagn* and five soldiers had charged into their home, looking for her husband, they found her listening to a tape of a *tegadelti* song. One of the soldiers knew our language, Tigrinya, so she was charged with being a sympathizer and brought to the *ghebi* a week before I turned up in her cell. Left behind with a maid were Berekti's three children, ages nine, seven, and four years old. When her husband, who was in Massawa at the time, heard that Berekti was in jail and that he was wanted himself, he had no choice but to join the Resistance.

Berekti told me that she had visited Mesfun and the children just before her arrest. Ruth and Tamar had grown very mature, she reported, but I was very disturbed to hear that she had sensed Muzit's worry and fear. I tried not to be emotional; in prison it is essential that you control your emotions, and I had so far succeeded in suppressing the longing for my children. I was hungry for news, any kind of news — about friends, relatives, the state of the country, and above all our dear *tegadelti*.

Like all the prisoners, Berekti and I agreed that it was an honor to be detained for the cause of freeing the motherland. Berekti was confident that her sister and her niece — my friend — would help with the children. She too had quickly learned to suppress her feelings for her family.

Berekti said it was her opinion that Colonel Mengistu, head of the Dergue, was hoping that the ELF and the EPLF would destroy each other so that he would not have to use the millions of dollars worth of armaments that he had procured from Russia.

My husband and I had worked closely with the churches during the days of our relief organization, and Berekti told me that members of several congregations had been praying for my release and that friends were holding prayer meetings in their homes. I was touched.

The best news, though, was that despite their intensive propaganda, the Dergue's army was encountering resistance wherever it went. Berekti told me that her grandmother in Keren fervently believed that St. Mary and St. Micael would protect the *tegadelti* and was encouraging everybody she knew to cooperate with them. Her grandmother was very old, Berekti said, but she was determined not to die before she saw a free and independent Eritrea.

Berekti was interrogated once — beaten over the shoulders with a heavy stick. She denied having had anything to do with the fronts and knowing anything about the underground activities of her husband. The authorities found out that the tape she had been listening to was being sold in the market, but they were capable of giving to it whatever meaning they wanted.

I was so happy to be with Berekti and so excited by all her news that I did not feel exhausted from the trauma of the day. It was only after I lay down that my body began to ache, and that night I had dreamt a dream — which according to prison mysticism meant that a rough time lay ahead for me.

In my half-awake and half-asleep state, early in the morning, I heard the cell lock rattle and sensed that the call would be for me. Berekti was fast asleep. One of the other women woke and helped me to stand and put on my *netsela* when she saw me struggling. The guard brought me outside into the courtyard and handed me over to the chief guard, the Sergeant, who was pacing up and down in the compound near the office. It was chilly at that hour, and the cool breeze brushing against my face, hands, and legs helped me to fully wake up.

"Good morning," said the Sergeant gravely.

"The Major called me twice during the night," he continued, standing face to face with me in the open air. "I'm sure you can guess why. I begged him to give you one last chance. For the sake of your children, confess and save your life. Can you not see how lenient they have been with you? I hate to see you go to the gallows. When I was assigned to the lowlands I used to give a little money to the rebels, because if I refused they would have killed me. So if I — an Ethiopian soldier — was forced to pay, it is understandable that you would be afraid not to cooperate. The authorities are mad at you not because you helped but because you are trying to conceal an open secret. I guarantee that if you confess nothing serious will happen to you."

I listened attentively and mustered every bit of strength I had in order to speak.

"Sergeant, thank you for your help and concern. If there was a confession to make, I would have made it the day I set foot in this place, but there is none; all the charges are false. Just do me a favor. Let me telephone my husband to say goodbye and to ask him to send me a Bible."

He did not say a word. We walked toward the office and he opened the door for me, and I went in.

It was half past six when I telephoned home, and Mesfun answered. My heart was heavy, for I had terrible news for him, but I sensed his pleasure when he heard my voice. I did not want to make it too painful for him. I just briefed him about what had happened and told him that I would probably be executed and asked him to send me a Bible as soon as possible.

Mesfun's voice dropped and there was total silence for a second. Then, collecting himself, he said:

"I know you have committed no crime, and they will not kill you. But if you confess to something you have not done in order to save yourself, you are signing your own death warrant. I will send you the Bible, but I want you to know that family and friends everywhere are praying for your release."

There was a pause.

"Life without you has no meaning for me," he continued. "I am doing everything possible to get you back home to the children and me."

We both hung up but my hands were left hanging in mid-air. I immediately controlled the rush of emotion I had felt when I heard my husband's voice.

I sensed right away that the Sergeant regretted having allowed me to make the call, and he warned me never to tell my interrogators or the Major about it. I could not understand why he had given me permission in the first place. Without another word, he took me not to my new cell with Berekti but back to my original cell. Fana and Saba were still asleep but the others were up. I had been happy to see Berekti, but it was good to be back with my old cellmates.

As my husband would tell me later, as soon as he hung up he dressed and drove toward the Palace. It was as though he believed a magic wand had rendered him invisible and that he would be able to pass through those huge, heavily-guarded iron gates, sweep me up, and carry me off to safety. But then he stopped short in the deceptively beautiful garden just outside the gates and gazed ahead blankly. He finally came to his senses, and the next thought that entered his head was to go to his office and ask one of the American vice-consuls to get him an appointment with the military governor of Eritrea, General Getachow Nadow.

The pompous governor was widely considered to have the mentality of an adolescent. He had been promoted from colonel to general just in time to be appointed governor — a reward for having succeeded in temporarily quelling revolts in the lowlands by resorting to mass slaughter.

He was furious when he received the call from the

American vice-consul, but nonetheless replied: "The husband of one of our prisoners wants to talk to me about his wife? Okay, send him over."

Mesfun had thought it would be far more expedient to obtain an appointment via the consulate, for it could have taken days to get through on his own. But his plan backfired. After he had driven to the governor's office and waited for hours, General Getachow bellowed:

"What do you think the Americans will do to me? They cannot even help their own citizens, let alone you. This is treason. We have repeatedly warned you to stay away from your wife's case. Guard, take this man to the prison!" His four bodyguards dragged Mesfun out of the governor's office and forced him into a jeep.

At about one in the afternoon, one of our guards asked me the name of my husband. This, coming after the telephone call I had made, left me feeling uneasy and downhearted. At four o'clock we heard a commotion in the corridor.

The guards would very occasionally open our cell door a crack to let us get a breath of air, and it so happened that this was one of those days: I saw with my own eyes what I had been secretly dreading all afternoon — my own husband being dragged into the cell directly opposite ours and rudely being ordered to remove his shoes and his belt.

"Oh, no! Not you, Mesfun. Not you!" I shouted.

My cellmates were dumbfounded. "Maybe... Oh, I'm sure it's... it must be just someone who looks like him...." said Ribka.

"It is him, definitely. Even if I had lost my mind, I would always recognise Mesfun."

Semhar helped me to wrap my *netsela* around my waist so that it would give support to my back. I opened the door wide, and there was the Sergeant — the Sergeant who had slyly tried to lure me into confessing, who had let me use the office telephone.

"Sergeant, let me greet my husband," I demanded.

"He is a prisoner like yourself now. That is what they were trying to tell you. Confession, lady, confession — it is the answer to everything, the only solution." His tone was icy.

I was beside myself with anger. I became hysterical. I forgot that I was an inmate and shouted: "How could you be so cruel

— to bring him here right in front of me and yet not let me talk to him? Why did you not put him in another cell where I would not be able to see him? Don't you have a mother... a wife... a sister?"

Then I went out of the cell door and walked towards Mesfun's cell.

One of the guards grabbed me by the hand.

"Leave me alone," I screamed.

"Leave her alone," ordered the Sergeant, and the guard pulled back immediately.

The Sergeant made a sign to the guard near the open door of Mesfun's cell and my husband simply walked out.

Our hands went around each other and my head rested on his chest. Tears of anguish ran down my cheeks. "Look what I have done to you," I said.

"It's okay," Mesfun whispered in my ear. "Just stick to what you have been saying. You have no confession to make. I see this as a God-given opportunity — how else could I have seen you? After all these weeks of grief and loneliness, now I can hold you in my arms."

His soothing words were like cool water in a desert. "Continue to be brave, and we shall both come out together," Mesfun said. "Don't worry about the children — they are doing just fine in the care of their grandparents."

The Sergeant ordered us to separate. It is astonishing how I found the energy to hang on so tight; finally, two guards had to forcibly pull us apart.

My cellmates were sobbing when I was thrown back to them. It must have been a pathetic sight — the reunion of a husband and wife, not in the privacy of their own home but in the corridor of a prison under armed guard and in the shadow of death.

The roller-coaster events of the day all conspired to aggravate my illness. Pain in every fiber of my body kept me wide awake the whole night, and in the opposite cell I could hear my husband clearing his throat time and again, confirmation that he was right there with me — just a few feet away yet separated from me by two heavy iron doors. There were already seven prisoners in Mesfun's cell, so he could not even find a patch of concrete to lie down. It was a sordid night. One more episode in my prison experience.

The next morning they transferred Mesfun to a building on our right where there were about seventy prisoners in one hall. Throughout the day, his gentle whisper — "You will be alright. How proud I am of you, that you are surviving such conditions. How happy I am to hold you in my arms. God's ways are mysterious. Be calm. We will come out together" — the words kept ringing in my ears, washing over my soul. That night I slept well.

On the fourth day after Mesfun's arrival at the *ghebi*, my cellmates and I were on our way to the toilet when for some reason I glanced in the direction of the large room to our left, which held some hundred prisoners. The door was open, and there, talking to another prisoner, was my father!

My feet almost shot out from under me. I thought the sky had fallen. The two most important men in my life were here, with me, in this hell.

"*Abboi*, why did you have to come? This is not a place for you," I burst out when I got back to our cell.

Their mother, their father, and also their grandfather — in prison. Now it really was time to worry about my children.

# Six

Mother rarely expressed her love with words, but she made sure that we all ate properly, studied diligently, and behaved, and she loved us dearly. Since I was the eldest of nine and had to set a good example, she was particularly strict with me. I helped with all the children, with the exception of the next two in line, Petros and Paulos, and the youngest of us all, Lia. A wonderful homemaker herself, Mother made me help the maids with the cooking and the cleaning after school and weekends — this on top of helping with the children daily. The discipline would serve me well later in life, of course, but how I wished then that Mother would be more lenient!

Nevertheless, I still preferred Mother's stick to Father's gentle approach. If I did something foolish, he might simply say, "I don't know why you did that, I don't expect that kind of behavior from you. Never do it again." And I would feel guilty. *Abboi* wasn't the hard-liner that *Addei* was, but I was always more careful not to disappoint him. He worked hard to provide a good life for his family. He quit his job with an Italian-owned shoe company to start his own business when I was seventeen, and he ran the family farm as well. My father believed in giving his children the best education possible.

There was something remarkable about the man. Everybody loved him. I shall never forget the day he took me for a ride on his bicycle, I must have been about seven. I was frightened when he put me on the crossbar, but *Abboi* said, "I was much older than you when I first rode a bicycle with a friend. Do you know what I did when we were going downhill? I screamed. But look how brave you are, the second time you come riding with me, you'll be just fine." I had no choice but to be brave! When he bought a motorcycle, I was the first to ride with him. With my hands around his waist, the wind blowing through my hair, I thought everyone in Arbate Asmara, our district, was watching us and saying, "What a lucky girl she is."

There was no father like mine, I thought.

Then when I grew up we became best friends. My marriage did not take me far from Abboi — I just moved to another neighborhood.

Father had been in prison four days before I saw him. He had caught a glimpse of me twice during our toilet visits, making sure that I did not see him even though their hall was overcrowded and the door was forever being opened and closed. When he found out that I knew he was there, he sent me a secret note. It went something like this:

"My dear daughter, my firstborn, my pride, my friend: There is a time for everything, a time for sorrow and a time for joy, a time for work and a time for rest; and definitely there will be a time when all of us will be free. Just keep your faith. I left the children in good hands, so don't worry about them. I saw Mesfun briefly during the toilet visit. We exchanged glances, but were not allowed to speak. I love you, my baby, my dear one.... Your Father."

When I read this, I fell apart. Every moment we had had together flashed before my eyes. I began to worry even more about my mother's precarious situation, my children, my two younger brothers, and my sister Lia.

*Addei's* sheltered world crumbled quickly. First her daughter was taken away, then her son-in-law, and finally her husband! It was when she was left with only her three youngest children and her grandchildren that she began to be alarmed. She was gripped with the fear of never seeing us again. She even entertained the possibility that my brothers and sisters abroad would never return. Vivacious, ever hopeful Mother, who dreamed of being a grandmother not of four but of forty, joined the countless other mothers affected by the war. She had always been too busy raising children and keeping house to venture out much, but when this tragedy befell her she began visiting other mothers, to console and be consoled.

The morning after I had seen my father I was called once

more to the Major's office, accompanied this time not by two guards, but by three. When I stepped into the office, there was my father, with his hands behind his back, looking dishevelled, his beard all stubbly. He was standing about five feet from where the Major sat.

I didn't ask permission to greet my father. I just ran and threw myself into his arms. It was so painful to see *Abboi*, my idol, in that wretched place. With tears choking him, he kept repeating, "It will be alright, daughter. It will be alright. God is with us." They didn't pull us apart as they did to Mesfun and me, and there were no harsh words from the Major or my two interrogators who sat on either side of him.

Finally, the Major ordered us to sit. We sat on the two chairs reserved for us, firmly clutching each other's hands. My interrogators looked at me as though they were spectators. Addressing my father formally, the Major proceeded:

"Your daughter is challenging the mighty Ethiopian revolutionary government. So far, we have been lenient with her, considering the fact that she is the mother of four children and in poor health. But she mistook our humane treatment for weakness. You are here to advise her to confess, to tell the truth, and then the higher authorities will have mercy on her. Give your daughter your honest advice, if you want her spared."

*Abboi* listened attentively and then began. "Major, I know my daughter well, for I have raised her. Whatever she has said must be the truth. If she said she has nothing to confess, it means she has none."

Glancing at me, he continued: "Daughter, are you not speaking the truth?" Our eyes met and we pressed our hands harder. And of course my reply was clear: "Yes."

At this point the Major took on the face and eyes of a beast.

"You Eritreans — elders, fathers, mothers, children — you are all rebels! We have a charge against you. Your rebel son Petros, with your consent, used your farm in Centro to hide rebels and arms. Your son Paulos in America has your blessing in his rebel activities there. You are a family of rebels. Damn you all.

"Interrogator! Take this man to the interrogation room and beat him. Throttle him until he confesses. He is the main rebel. There will be no mercy for this family."

Both interrogators stood up. I held *Abboi* by the waist and cried out with all my might: "You can't do that to my father. Beat me to death if you want, but don't touch *Abboi*."

"The Lord will give me strength, daughter. Don't worry about me. Let us trust Him." He was remarkably calm as he took my hands away.

Suddenly the Major changed his mind. He ordered the two guards to take us back to our cells.

My husband was watching as my father and I were being dragged from the office, for they had let the inmates out in order to spray their hall, which was infested with bugs and lice. Mesfun was shaking from head to toe — he was afraid we had fallen into the Major's trap.

Of the many times, in the next four days, that I tried to catch a glimpse of my father on our way to the toilets, I succeeded only twice. But I had no news whatsoever of Mesfun. There was always the possibility that he had been transferred to Sembel Prison. Despite the peace of mind that Mesfun's being nearby had brought me, I felt very uneasy about him and I visualized our children in emotional turmoil.

One particularly hot day, the eighth day after his arrival, one of the food messengers, a prisoner from Mesfun's hall, came into our cell to hand Fana her food parcel. As he did so, he said: "Abeba, I have a note for you from Mesfun. I'll give it to you when I can."

I could hardly contain myself for the few minutes that I had to wait for my parcel. Tsegga's name was called, and finally it was my turn. As the messenger handed me my lunch, stepping inside the cell, he loosened his shirtsleeve and a gold-colored folded cigarette paper fell out. He left immediately, calling out the name of the next food-parcel recipient.

The guards were always on the lookout while food parcels were being delivered. I could not read the note while the door was open, yet the light was so dim after the door had been closed that I still could not read it. Evening came. As usual, the doors were checked twice at night by the guards. We said our prayers. Then I was free to light our candle and see what was in that tiny gold cigarette paper all folded up looking like a candy.

There were no secrets among us cellmates. I shared the note

with all the women, and that small cigarette paper had a very soothing message.

"I have a feeling you are worrying about the children,"
Mesfun began. "Have no fear, they will be fine. My brother is there
for them, and so are the other relatives and friends. I have a strong
feeling that the three of us will get out soon. Please try to relax and
eat as much as you can. You don't want the children to see you
just skin and bones."

Although I had been eating better and my health had
improved, I now decided to eat even more and to believe as he
did that we would soon be released. After reading his note over
and over, I hid it in my bra, close to my heart, in case a sudden
search was conducted. With his note Mesfun had enclosed a blank
cigarette paper, and when all my cellmates were asleep I wrote
him a reply. That little piece of paper wasn't nearly large enough,
so I had to resort to toilet paper — we had had to smuggle in two
pencils, a pen, and candles, but toilet paper and soap were permitted. The next day, the food messenger took my letter to deliver it to Mesfun and gave me a second one!

Our correspondence continued for five days, and every
day our letters got longer and more passionate. The notes, written mostly on toilet paper, were not about our charges, prison life,
or news from the outside: they were expressions of our love and
commitment to one another. "To the most beautiful and pure of
women"; "To my darling whose eyes are dove-like and whose
steps are majestic"; "To my friend and the mother of my children";
"To my very life and queen of my heart" was how his letters would
begin! He made me feel like I was queen of queens! My letters to
him were equally romantic. We longed to be together, we wanted
to talk, to hold hands.

At the Palace Prison, where madness, terror, and death are
the order of the day, where the environment is anything but kind
to the senses, I discovered a new love with my own husband, a
romance that I had not even known when we were young and
courting: because no matter how modern and progressive he might
be in other ways, an Eritrean husband does not verbally express
his love to his wife. And while an Eritrean woman might be liberated to some extent, tradition dictates that when it comes to
expressing her emotions she must always be modest and demure.

If I had the talent of an artist, I wrote to Mesfun, I would sculpt him perfectly — his shoulders, those strong, veined hands of his, his torso, even the little hairs on his chest. I can hardly believe now that it was my very own hand that put to paper words of such passionate abandon. How I wished then that we could return with this new, uninhibited love of ours to the places around the world we had visited together — to the balcony of our hotel room in Rome, where the summer evening breeze does wonders for the soul — to the festive atmosphere of historic Copenhagen — to the sidewalk cafés of Paris — to exotic Karachi — to the canal bridges of Amsterdam where lovers stroll — to that beautiful hotel in Bangkok, near the Buddhist temple with its golden dragons — to the opera house near the water in faraway Sydney, Australia — to the ancient pyramids of Egypt — to the beautiful home of our friend in Nairobi — to the exquisite gardens of Switzerland — to the long, stately corridors of the Prado in Madrid — to the Acropolis in Athens — to the magnificent parks in Washington DC — even to the privacy of our own bedroom, or our beautiful garden when the servants had their day off and our daughters were with their grandparents.

Mesfun gained a little weight within a week, and my own health improved beyond belief. Hope and vitality began once again to course through my veins. Our correspondence was like an oasis in a desert of darkness and fear. It did me a world of good. For a few short days, I was oblivious to all the suffering that went on in that awful place.

Five remarkable days passed in this state of utter fantasy, but reality was beckoning.

On the sixth day, I was not in my cell to receive Mesfun's note. I was called for interrogation just before the lunch roll call. By then I was much steadier on my feet and did not require assistance. As the guard led me through the compound on the way to the interrogation room, I saw what at first appeared to be a corpse; but then I could see that although the man lay motionless he was at least alive. His face was black and blue, and so incredibly swollen that his eyes were completely closed; they looked like two brown eggs. His feet were like balloons about to burst. His white shirt was covered in blood. His thick hair was in disarray.

I was shaken from head to toe. White shirt and green pants

— the uniform of Ethiopian Airlines! Who could it be? I wondered. Then the forehead and hair gave me a clue. It was one of our ticket agents, Teame Adhanom! I would later learn that he had been arrested the previous day and beaten for hours. Teame was young, handsome, and defiant, and the interrogators harbored a particularly deep hatred for such qualities in an Eritrean man.

My interrogator, the vicious younger one, led me into the interrogation room. Before I had even settled into my usual chair, he pulled his chair over to me quickly, sat down, and began: "That boy outside..."

He is not a boy, I thought, he is a man. *A man with guts.*

"You know him. Right? He is an arrogant Ethiopian Airlines employee. During interrogation he gave us six names, all EPLF underground cell members. He is going to testify against you. Three charges, woman, three charges: collecting money from businessmen and forwarding it to the rebels through your brother Petros; redirecting relief funds, clothing, supplies, and food; and being an active member of an Ethiopian Airlines cell of the EPLF. Now your case is more complicated than ever!"

I did not respond. It was all I could do to hide my emotion and keep myself under a modicum of control. The interrogator left me alone for about an hour — to this day I cannot figure out why — and then returned and dismissed me. He stood on the stairs and surveyed me as a guard took me back to my cell. Teame was no longer lying in the compound on my return.

Is the interrogator just telling lies, as usual? I wondered. Surely Teame would not betray me! No, I knew he wouldn't. The pathetic sight of his bruised and battered body haunted me for days. I visualised my father and Mesfun in that state, and I also had to face up to the fact that now that my health was improved, I could very well be subjected to physical torture myself. These dark thoughts were short-lived, though. I quickly dismissed them from my mind. Come what may, we had no choice but to endure whatever lay in store.

That same day, Fana was in turmoil. She missed her son almost to the point of insanity and was in the mood to criticize the leadership of the ELF and its network in Asmara. Ribka, who was a member of Fana's organisation, disagreed with her. Tsegga, in the meantime, had not received a lunch parcel for three days and was worried that her aunt had either abandoned her or been arrested herself. Semhar and Tsegga got into a serious argument.

My clandestine communication with Mesfun had come to a halt. I was beside myself with worry.

One thing after another kept happening in those four days. The worst was the night of the third day.

Once the main entrance and the cell doors were locked for the night, there was very little movement within the prison. On that particular night, the worry of not hearing from Mesfun, and the increasing discord among the women in my cell, kept me awake the whole night. It was well past midnight when I heard the big entrance door being opened. The heavy steps of a guard came nearer and nearer until they stopped near our cell. I woke my cellmates just before the door to our cell was flung open.

"Abeba," the guard shouted.

We all froze.

I remembered what my interrogator had said during my last interrogation three days before. So this was it. They were going to execute me... but why at night?

Images flashed through my mind: Mesfun and *Abboi* being left to grieve in prison; my poor daughters — their mother dead, their father and grandfather locked away in prison; my mother mourning the death of her first-born alone, her husband in jail.

A pungent smell pervaded the cell, and with it came a terrible human odor. The guard was completely drunk.

Before he had been imprisoned, Mesfun had used the connections of his position to press for my release. This tall young guard was the one who had smuggled in a pen and pencil, candles, and needle and thread for me. Mesfun had told him about my case, and he was secretly sympathetic. The guard had gotten drunk, and now he had come to make a social call!

But the horror of it all was over in minutes. The Sergeant grabbed the young man by the collar and hauled him away.

At the end of four days, the tension subsided. Tsegga and Semhar reconciled. Fana stopped fuming about the inadequacies of the movement and began to come to terms with her situation. She frequently repeated her condemnation of the Ethiopians: "*Deki sheramuth meshemish Amhara tetzawitenalei*," albeit with less rancor. Ribka grew more tolerant of poor Fana, realizing that she desperately needed our understanding and support. Tsegga's food parcels began coming again six days after they had ceased. Prayer helped us get through those dark days.

Most significant for me, my secret communication with Mesfun resumed. Our accommodating food messenger had been transferred, and it took some persuading before his replacement, who was from my father's hall, would take on the task. Later, I even sent a note to *Abboi*, and was rewarded with a reply.

The fifth morning after her confession, Fana folded her blanket and gathered together her few belongings. We were all in tears as she bade us goodbye and went off to Haz Haz Prison for Women to await trial.

The letter that I received from Mesfun after he had been in jail for three weeks contained special news.

"This is too good to be true!" I said as I handed it to Ribka to read. He and my father were going to be released the next day! The entire little cell went wild with joy. We acted like children, shouting and screaming until the guards came to see what was going on. When I heard footsteps approaching our cell, I immediately chewed up Mesfun's letter; it did not take much for a piece of toilet paper to melt in my mouth. I had sewn all his earlier letters into the hem of a pair of pants that I never sent home to be washed.

The day before their release, the two were summoned to the luxurious offices of the governor. After preaching about the clemency being shown by the Ethiopian military government, the General told my husband and my father that because there were three members of one family involved, it had been decided to grant them mercy. But he strictly warned Mesfun to never again meddle in my case. Ruthless as he was known to be, the governor never missed an opportunity to display a paternalistic concern for his subjects.

The next day, my cellmates and I got up very early. The daily routine of the prison commenced. We went to the toilet and with a half gallon of water I had a bath in our usual prison fashion — very hastily, one of my friends holding my shirt and keeping watch. On our way back we all washed our faces. We folded the blankets and placed them to the sides of the cell, then we swept the floor and sat on the folded blankets. Usually, no one much cared to eat breakfast from the leftovers of the previous day, which were placed outside in the corridor due to lack of space. But that morning we happily ate it all up.

With a faint glimmer of hope that I would be allowed to see my husband and my father being released, I dressed and used whatever means available to look my very best. And, yes, luckily they relented and gave us the chance to say goodbye to each other!

It was on a Saturday morning around eleven when I met *Abboi* and Mesfun in the courtyard, supervised by the Major himself and a few guards. The weather was perfect: brilliant sunshine, the sky an endless sea of blue, an ever-so-gentle breeze. The flowers were in full bloom, and it seemed to me that I had never before seen grass so green. In the huge palace compound, horses and cows grazed without a care in the world. When I walked hand-in-hand with Mesfun and *Abboi* I felt that we were in paradise itself, that heaven and earth had cooperated to help me celebrate the freedom of my loved ones. It was hard to believe that amid such beauty, in the stable where horses had once been groomed with loving care, men were now terrorizing and torturing their fellow human beings, the people of Eritrea.

At the threshold of the gates, *Abboi* pressed my hands into his and said, "Have courage." But as he was about to leave I could not help but notice the pain in his eyes.

"Either I'll get you out of this or I'll be back inside," said Mesfun with suppressed anger in his voice. "I cannot rest with my better half in prison." It was a miracle that our guards were at that moment standing just out of earshot.

As the guards escorted me out of the courtyard and back to my cell, I saw Mesfun and *Abboi* go out through the garden and disappear.

# Seven

Mesfun was not in his office — on the day of my imprisonment — when the telephone operator at Ethiopian Airlines called the American consulate to tell him about my being taken away. So she left a message and then called my father. Mesfun told me later that the first thing he and my father did was check with all the prisons. By late afternoon they knew I was being held at the Palace Prison.

My husband was unusually late getting home that night, for he spent some time with my parents. He slipped unnoticed into the house and went up to our bedroom so as not to let the children see him arrive without their mother. He then tried to call the children through the telecom. They were downstairs where we had taken to spending most of our time. He could not bring himself to press the button. Trying his best to look calm, he went downstairs and not giving the girls a chance to ask of my whereabouts, he summoned Ruth and Tamar to follow him.

When they faced their father in the dining room, Ruth and Tamar sensed that something was wrong. Instead of beating around the bush, he decided, it would be best to be direct.

"Your mother is not coming home tonight. The *afagn* took her from her work. But at least we know she is safe at the Palace."

As they began asking questions, Mesfun realized that our two sheltered children had turned into brave, well-informed young women, even if tears were streaming down their cheeks.

The three of them decided then to keep the news to themselves. Muzit and Senait were told that I had been called to a meeting in Addis Ababa at the last minute, and everyone who came to the house was warned to stick to this story. Muzit and Senait thought it odd that I had not even telephoned them, and the reactions of their teachers and some of their classmates made them suspect that I had gone not to Addis Ababa but to some awful place.

Ruth took on a motherly role, and, being a great reader, she read to the younger ones and told them stories. Tamar has always loved children and she delighted in taking care of her sisters. Muzit and Senait began to look up to their sisters.

When Mesfun and my father were thrown in jail, however, it was impossible to keep up the façade. Muzit and Senait had to be told. Their comfortable little world collapsed.

My mother was too broken-hearted herself to console her grandchildren. She did want them with her, but there was a general consensus that leaving their home might make the girls feel even more insecure, so my brother-in-law, Yohannes, went to stay with them. My brothers Dawit and Michael and my sister Lia were also there most of the time. Relatives, friends, and neighbors lavished their attention on the family, while Shashu, our maid, played a particularly vital role.

But all this kindness did not make the fears go away. Five o'clock was especially painful for all the girls, Shashu told me later. Senait would watch for her Papa's steps with a special look of hopefulness in her eyes. Some women cried openly when they came to visit. It was all so confusing. Trying to be brave for the sake of their little sisters was difficult for Ruth and Tamar.

This was a grim time for the city of Asmara, going from grey to black. There was more fear and more talking in hushed tones behind closed doors.

The release of my husband and my father came as a complete surprise to everybody. When they arrived home, *Abboi* blew his horn at the gate, but *Addei* and her help refused to open it. Who could it be, they wondered? Who are they going to take next? A visiting relative peeped through a hole in the gate, finally, and saw that it was my father behind the wheel.

My mother had just been preparing the lunch parcels for the three of us. After joyously hugging her husband and son-in-law, she was gripped by fear and anxiety and the words tumbled out: "Where is my daughter?" *Abboi* lowered his eyes, while Mesfun murmured, "She has been kept behind." Her face darkened and there was total silence. As Mesfun squared his shoulders and prepared to leave, *Addei*, feeling guilty for not thanking the Lord for the wonderful blessing, said, "Mesfun, stay here with us. I'll have the children brought over right away." But Mesfun wanted to get his daughters himself.

My mother telephoned to tell Shashu that Mesfun was on his way. They all ran to the gate, of course, and at the sight of their father they went wild. The children could not believe their eyes. They kissed him and hugged him and laughed and cried with joy.

But they were puzzled. They wanted to see their Papa and Mommy together, just like the good old days. As though they had rehearsed it, they all asked in unison, "Where's Mommy? Why didn't you bring her?"

Saddened because he was not able to tell the girls what they wanted to hear, Mesfun said, "They couldn't release her today... but we're hoping she won't be there much longer. She sends her love and kisses to all of you.

"And here's more good news: Your grandfather is out too! Grandma told me how well you have been handling the situation and how brave you all have been. Get ready. We are all going to visit your grandparents."

"Papa, did the prison people let you have some time with Mommy?" Tamar asked.

"Oh, yes. We had a good twenty minutes this morning," he replied. "They let me see her for a moment when they first detained me, and twice I saw her from a distance."

"Papa, did you have a good place to sleep?" Muzit asked him.

"There was no problem, darling. It was not bad at all."

"What about Mommy? How does she look?" she continued.

"We had lots of candy when you were away," interrupted Senait. "We didn't buy it, people brought it to us. I told them you don't allow us to eat candy, but they wanted us to have it anyway."

Ruth was more serious: "What was your charge, Papa?" and "Why did Mommy have to stay behind?"

Mesfun's aunt was visiting at the time and she assured the children that I too would soon be free, but Ruth and Tamar feared that my case would not be as simple as their father's and their grandfather's had been.

Mesfun showered and changed, and then they all rushed

back to my parents' house.

     Word quickly spread, and all day until curfew time people streamed in to join the half-hearted celebrations.

# Eight

As the guard motioned for me to return to my cell the morning I bade farewell to my husband and my father, I made a solemn vow never to think about myself now that they were released. The freedom of every prisoner in our nation was inevitable someday, I was sure.

After Mesfun's release, we began corresponding through a tea thermos. We would hide the letter between the two cups that served as a cover, which did not come apart easily. Every day I would receive a thermos full of tea, and there would be Mesfun's letter and a blank piece of paper for my note. Each day, the empty thermos returned to my family with my reply.

After two weeks of this, the thermos — our postman in disguise — broke during inspection. Word reached that the note had been discovered. Miraculously, the guard brought the note to me instead of playing the hero and showing it to his supervisor.

"I found this letter in your thermos," said the guard, standing in the doorway of our cell. "I can't read it. [It was written in Tigrinya.] What does it say? Who sent it to you?"

"This is a note from my husband," I replied, trying hard to keep my knees from giving out.

"Don't you know he could be brought back and severely punished? Go ahead and read it for me," the guard said sternly but without hostility. I read out only the greeting, translating it into Amharic. "You can understand how he feels after being here with me for three weeks. He misses me just like I miss him. There is no harm in it," I said.

He smiled and I could feel my parched lips cracking. Under normal circumstances, never would a guard pass a smuggled letter discovered during inspection along to its addressee. I can only say it was a miracle.

"Okay, but if he does it again, even if it's just a 'hello," said the guard, "it could get you both into big trouble." He walked away, leaving me with the letter in my hand.

I read it once again very quickly, then hastily chewed it up and swallowed it. "What a relief!" I said to my cellmates.

The letter read:

"My dear: Yesterday, we had a number of visitors, mostly relatives, bringing with them sweets for the children. Senait must wonder why they are being pampered so much. Ruth and Tamar are helping Shashu to run the house as well as mothering their sisters. They all love the constant flow of visitors, but they want their mother too. Despite the good time we had with the guests and my hope that you will soon be released, I had a sleepless night. Something is still bothering me: I heard that interrogators have found a much more subtle way to lure prisoners into signing pre-arranged confessions, thereby getting the military court to sentence them to fifteen and twenty years. I left you in good spirits and full of courage, and I pray that you will continue like this until we are together again. But let me say one thing: If I were you I would rather die than sign a pre-arranged confession and rot in prison. I love you with all my heart and I'm exploring every avenue to have you released. Whenever you feel depressed, just think about people who are less fortunate than yourself. My regards to your cellmates... Mesfun."

If this letter had fallen into the wrong hands, it would have spelled the end of us both!

Think about others, Mesfun had told me. But didn't I always think about others? And even if I did take his advice to heart, what could I do here, under lock and key?

Then a certain man came to mind. I hated him for his irresponsible and stupid actions, for having defected to the Dergue, for believing that the prison lords would be lenient with him for collaborating with them — for causing my ordeal as well as betraying his motherland.

The object of my rancor was the Eritrean man who had testified against me when he, Ato Tesfai Woldemichael the businessman and I had all been brought before the interrogators together.

In fact, he himself had been an EPLF agent responsible for collecting money from certain donors. And indeed on one occasion when he had approached Ato Tesfai for his contribution, he was told that the money had already been given to me to pass along to Petros. He was speaking not to a committed member of the EPLF, unfortunately, but to a man who would later defect to the enemy. But I had faith in Ato Tesfai. I knew he would neither betray me nor get caught in their trap. Ato Tesfai was eventually given five years in prison, while the informer was sentenced to twenty since he had been an actual agent of the EPLF.

What my grandmother had taught me about the virtue of forgiving one's enemies was deeply ingrained in me. I had told my cellmates the story of Irène Laure forgiving the Germans who had caused death and destruction upon her country. I had smugly thought that it should be no more difficult for them to forgive each other than it had been for Irène Laure to forgive the Germans. Now I had to practise what I preached.

Confronting people is never easy, but confronting oneself is even harder. I found it very, very difficult to forgive this man. If he had not told them about my collecting money for the front, the *afagn* would never have known about my involvement in the EPLF. They had only been guessing that I was an active member of the Ethiopian Airlines underground cell.

Hard as it was for me to forgive this contemptible informer, however, that night I made the firm decision that I *would* forgive him — and I resolved to tell him about my decision the next time we met.

Two days later, we met at the outdoor faucet. I made it brief:

"That morning you shamelessly testified against me on just hearsay... as a committed underground member of the EPLF, I hated your guts. Now I forgive you. If it were not for these horrendous times, neither you nor I, nor any of our cellmates, would be here in prison."

The man seemed shocked. He lowered his head and said nothing. I left him quickly and caught up with my cellmates. A sense of great peace swept over me. Time and again, he came to our cell to convince me to confess. He was still being used by the enemy.

The next day I was called for interrogation again, and the Major began: "I have personally done you a big favor. Despite pressure from the chief of security, I managed to have your father and your husband released. Now it's time for you to do me a favor."

"What kind of favor can you possibly expect from me — a prisoner?" I asked.

"Confess. Confess. You have three charges against you. There is no way you can deny them all. You would be wise to confess — it is your only salvation."

Mesfun's letter had been very timely indeed.

"Thank you for everything, Major, but I have no confession to make," I said firmly. Now that my father and my husband had been released, I didn't care what they did with me. They could detain me as long as they wanted.

The Major gazed at the ceiling as if deeply perturbed, and then looked back at me. "What do you do to stubborn people, people you try to help but who refuse to help themselves?" By that time, of course, I knew that lying and play-acting were an integral part of prison interrogation, so I made no response.

"Woman," he continued, "as far as I'm concerned, the interrogation is over. Get ready to be transferred to Haz Haz Prison until we receive further instructions from the chief of security and the governor himself. I'm warning you that there could be very grave consequences, so don't blame me for what happens. I have done everything possible to help you."

Just as the Major was about to call a guard to take me back to my cell, I asked him when I would be going to Haz Haz. "As soon as a car is available," he snapped. "It could be tomorrow. It could be now." But ten days would pass before the transfer took place.

Of all the occurrences at the Palace Prison during those next ten days, three in particular stand out in my memory.

The first occurrence was Semhar's release. Yes, intelligent and witty Semhar was set free! We were overjoyed more than words can express, yet we missed her terribly. Semhar did just what all her cellmates expected she would do: instead of going back to her mother and her brothers, she joined the EPLF, and became a fighter, a *tegalalit*.

The second notable event at the Palace during those ten days was the imprisoning of a mother with her three children, ranging in age from seven months to four years. The woman's husband had been an active member of an EPLF cell, along with her brother who lived with them. When the two men heard that the *afagn* were looking for them, they were compelled to flee. Two days later, while she was still consumed with worry over their sudden disappearance, the *afagn* descended upon the woman's home and, with their usual crudeness, ransacked it. In the absence of the two men, they took the poor woman and her three children.

As her cellmates would tell me later during our toilet visits, this woman was trembling like a leaf and had the eyes of a frightened animal when she was dragged into the cell. It was dusk when they burst into her home, and she had been baking *engera*; they did not even give her a chance to wash her hands.

Her four-year-old son, already unsettled by the disappearance of his father, began to cry the moment he was thrown into the cell. The first night in prison he kept saying *"Abboi*, where are you? Please come and take me home. *Abboi*, I love you. *Abboi*, I miss you" over and over. This wailing and fretting was so disquieting, so tormenting, that it even touched the hearts of some of the guards. At one point in the night, when the child's crying grew louder and more soulful, we inmates heard a cell door being opened. A guard attempted to console the little boy, even bringing him out into the corridor. But the child became more frantic. He wanted his father and his home, not a prison guard and a jail cell. When he finally cried for his mother, the guard returned him to the cell.

The next morning, an elderly guard opened the door of our cell for the morning toilet visit and said, *"Wutu"* — Get out. Shaking his head sadly, he muttered: "Oh Lord, why did you bring me to this hell? I came here to save Eritrea from being sold to the Arabs by a few irresponsible guerrillas, not to inflict suffering upon women and children. Where else on this earth of ours does a little child get arrested? Could this be the end of the world — doomsday?"

The sight of that thin, sickly boy I chanced to glimpse in the corridor will remain with me to the day I die. The family was set free after four days and nights from this nightmare.

The third, and for me the saddest experience was the sight of a *tegadalai* who had been captured in battle and brought to the *ghebi*. We prisoners generally sensed when something unusual was happening. The afternoon of the hero's arrival, there was great excitement among the officials and the guards. They made sure our doors were locked and they warned us that our afternoon toilet visit would be canceled that day. We could hear them pacing up and down the corridor, perhaps trying to decide which cell to put him in.

Just as the conscripted Ethiopian soldier cowers before the superior fighting ability and iron-like discipline of the dedicated Eritrean freedom fighter, the prison lords were extremely cautious in their handling of our new arrival — even though he was shackled and rendered helpless. And with good reason. Our freedom fighters are much revered: they not only choose suffering over comfort, they are willing to die for the cause of liberation so that future generations will be able to live in their motherland in peace. Had it not been for the selflessness, determination, and commitment of our fighters over these many years, the Dergue would have been more ruthless in its treatment of civilians. Anyone familiar with the Eritrean struggle marvels at how thirty to forty thousand lightly-armed freedom fighters can tie down as many as three hundred thousand soldiers armed with the very latest, most sophisticated weaponry supplied by the Soviet Union.

After four nights in a cell with five other inmates, the freedom fighter was transferred to Addis Ababa to be interrogated directly by the members of the Dergue. We later heard that he had been shot along with four other prisoners of war after undergoing a month of inhumane interrogation.

After exactly ten days — on a Tuesday morning — I was given five minutes to get ready for transfer to the Haz Haz Prison for Women. By this time, there was only one women's cell left at the Palace. Fana had been transferred and Semhar had been released. Berekti, had also been transferred, and her two cellmates had been moved in with us. Men were being imprisoned at an alarming rate, but the overall number of women in detention was no more than thirty at a time. By 1983, in contrast, there would be forty women at the Palace Prison alone, Haz Haz would be filled to the maximum, and another prison would open in Asmara, the

Mariam Ghimbi Prison for men and women.

My cellmates and I had grown so close that it was not without heartache that I left our tiny patch of concrete. With my bundle containing a blanket, a sheet, a sweater, a pair of pants, and a thermos — and mentally carrying all kinds of messages from my cellmates in the hope that I might soon be freed — I boarded the jeep that would take me to Haz Haz.

As I sat in the back seat beside the guard, I tried to momentarily forget that I was merely being moved from one prison to another so that I could enjoy the sights of my beautiful city. Since Asmara is small and I had lived my whole life there, I knew almost every street like the back of my hand; moreover, I knew so many of its inhabitants that I could hardly walk anywhere without greeting some friend or acquaintance. It was half past twelve when we left the Palace, and I was able to feast my eyes on the streets filled with workers on their lunch break and even catch a glimpse of children playing in a schoolyard. Once you are caged up in a prison you think that life has ground to a halt elsewhere as well, but here was the world going about its business as though nothing were wrong at all!

I tried to locate my old high school; I had loved school and all the fun that went with it. I thought of the endless discussions we used to have about the Eritrean issue. In 1958 and 1959 the students from our school, Prince Mekonen Secondary School, as well as those from Haile Selassie Secondary, held several strikes. The boys would often be arrested, but never the girls, even though we participated with equal fervor. There was always an excuse to go on strike — replacement of Tigrinya with Amharic as the language of learning, lack of proper textbooks — but our ultimate objective was always the same; independence for Eritrea. Even with all these burning issues, however, we had a good time. Being only a dozen girls among more than three hundred boys, we were the center of attention in high school. The fun we would have when our team won a soccer match, the laughter and the silliness — all came back to me as vividly as though only weeks had passed. It was a wonderful, nostalgic journey.

But in no time, unfortunately, the jeep pulled up to the gates of Haz Haz and I was handed over to my new jailers.

Haz Haz Prison for Women consisted of one big building

with two large rooms, two small rooms, a bathroom, and a corridor. Two smaller buildings contained offices. Barbed wire ran all along the top of the stone fence; but Haz Haz was less heavily guarded than the *ghebi* and it included an open area at the back where we could sit between seven in the morning and four in the afternoon. A handful of well-armed guards were posted outside. The inside guards were middle-aged Eritrean women, most of them the widows of Eritrean policemen or commandos.

Prisoners were not normally permitted to keep jewelery or other personal belongings. While my earrings and wristwatch had been taken upon my arrival at the Palace, luckily they had not noticed my wedding ring, which is inscribed with my husband's name and the date of our marriage and which was a great comfort to me. But the registrar at Haz Haz demanded that I surrender it. As I reluctantly handed over my ring, a memory came to mind of my mother's sparkling eyes and my father's smile when I had put on my wedding gown and bowed to kiss their knees to receive blessings, as our custom requires.

I quickly banished such sentimental thoughts from my mind, and followed the guard down a corridor to a room with a high ceiling and a small barred window. In contrast to the tiny, cramped cell at the Palace, this room was unbelievably spacious for the number of women who occupied it — fourteen in all. I would have preferred to have all my old cellmates set free, but it was nevertheless good to be reunited with Fana, Saba, and Berekti.

All but five of the thirty-one Haz Haz prisoners were accused of being confirmed members, collaborators, or sympathizers of the underground — either the ELF or the EPLF. One of them was serving a fifteen-year sentence, two ten years, and one five; the rest were either undergoing trial or awaiting their verdicts.

Haz Haz Prison for Women was quite unlike the Palace Prison. Most notably, it lacked the constant tension, since no interrogation was conducted. We were free at last from the ever-present threat of pain and torture and from the ploys of the Major. We were allowed to keep a Bible and to have relatives and friends visit — although our visitors were kept at a distance. The toilets were located inside the building and there was water for a bath.

My friendship with Saba, Fana, and Berekti continued, and

since we were free to mingle I made friends with almost all of the other inmates. I developed a special friendship with Sister Weini, the eldest of us all, who would have been around fifty-five, and Genet, who was about twenty-three years old.

Sister Weini was born during the Italian occupation of Eritrea. She was married when she was eleven years old, and although it was an arranged marriage, it developed into a union of mutual love and respect. This marital bliss would be short-lived, however. In order to increase the ranks of their army, the Italians mobilised *"Askaris"* — soldiers from the colonies — and Weini's husband was one of those called up to serve in the Italian invasion of Libya.

At war's end, the *Askaris* were sent back home. When the Eritrean conscripts returned they were welcomed home to Asmara with great fanfare. For those who found their men alive, it was a moment of joy and happiness. But for others there was only grief, and Weini was among the latter.

Weini continued to live with her in-laws for a year and then moved back with her parents. She did not like the idea of remarrying, but her relatives and the village elders — and even her in-laws — came to her parents' home every Sunday to dole out the same unsolicited advice: "Your husband was destined to die in that faraway land. We grieve for him and all those who died with him, but you have mourned long enough. God does not want you to waste your youth as a widow; you should remarry and have children."

Weini finally gave in and married for the second time.

At first Weini could not shake the memory of her late husband, and she refused to share the bed of her new husband. As time went by, however, she ceased to mourn, and began to enjoy a normal married life. She gave birth to two girls. Just as she was beginning to settle into a family life and to love her second husband, he suddenly died of a mysterious illness. Weini was twenty-six years old and her children were eight and six. Grief and melancholy took over her entire being. Later on she was pressed to marry for the third time, but this time Weini was infuriated by such social pressure and was determined to refuse. "I would rather give my neck to the hangman than marry for the third time," she would say.

The succeeding years were fraught with hardship, but Weini's parents and in-laws helped her with the farm. She saw her daughters through to the ages of fourteen and twelve, then married them off.

Relieved of family responsibilities, Weini made a serious decision: she would devote the rest of her life to serving God. She was illiterate, but the Bible had been taught to her by the Orthodox priests. She assumed the task of keeping the church clean and she began to help the older women in her parish. She spread the word to sick and disabled women and helped them with their housework. She was declared a nun after five years of service.

In most of the homes that Sister Weini visited, people were whispering about "our boys in the bush." In the early years of the struggle, the revered freedom fighters would take advantage of every opportunity — such as funerals and religious gatherings — to address the country people about their aims and objectives. Over the years, Sister Weini saw how they would secretly come to the villages and help the farmers with their ploughing, vaccinate their animals, and encourage them to fight illiteracy. Sister Weini herself was taught to read by the fighters, and a whole new world was opened to her: she was able to read the Bible herself. Her heart went out to the freedom fighters and what they stood for. She decided to help in any way that she could, primarily by baking bread for the *tegadelti* whenever they appeared in her village.

After every harvest, the farmers would take part of their produce to market and use the earnings to purchase staples such as coffee, salt, and sugar. On one such trip to Asmara, Sister Weini, carrying a heavy load on her back, joined three women from her village on the journey to town. They became so deeply engrossed in conversation that in no time they reached the military checkpoint of Asmara. Sister Weini had never encountered any difficulty before, and she and the soldiers exchanged greetings as usual. But this time, all four women were thoroughly searched.

The other three women were allowed to proceed with their sacks of peas and grain, but Sister Weini was detained. The soldiers had found *tegadelti* leaflets and other educational materials written in Tigrinya hidden in the load on her back. They could not believe their eyes. A complement of ten soldiers — two jeeps full

— appeared at the site immediately.

Sister Weini was taken to the Palace Prison and held for a week, then transferred to Haz Haz. The security people were astonished that a woman of her age — and a nun at that — would collaborate with the freedom fighters, who they considered to be devils with horns!

"Who gave you the bunch of leaflets and where were you taking them?" was the first question thrown at Sister Weini during her interrogation at the Palace. She had difficulty understanding Amharic, so they had to use an interpreter.

"I was just coming to town to buy oil for my lamp," she replied. "On my way, I saw a boy loaded down with two sacks so I offered to help. He was right behind us when I was stopped at the checkpoint."

"How long have you been rendering services to strangers on the road?" asked her interrogator.

"I always try to help people, but I cannot tell you exactly when, where, and how. Usually I'm in my village spreading the word of God to sick and disabled people in their homes."

"How often do the *shiftas* come to your village and assign tasks to you like the one you were doing the day you were arrested?"

"My son, I have never seen any *shiftas*," she replied.

This irritated the interrogator and he began calling her names. When the interpreter translated his tirade into Tigrinya, Sister Weini said:

"Hold your tongue, my son, don't talk like that. It's offensive to God to utter such vile words. I'm going to pray for your soul — just as soon as you let me out of here." She used such a grandmotherly tone on him that the interrogator somehow did not dare lift a finger against her.

After detaining Sister Weini for eight months, considering her age and believing that she had merely been used by the *tegadelti*, they would finally release her.

Fifty-five could hardly be considered old, but the difficult life that Sister Weini had led made her appear older than her years. She always had some delightful story to tell about the characters in her village or some interesting personal experience, and all the inmates loved her dearly.

"Believe in Him, and we will witness the Amharas leaving our country one morning, very soon," Sister Weini was fond of saying.

Genet, first-born of six, was only about five feet tall and weighed not more than ninety pounds when we met at the Haz Haz Prison for Women. When serious issues were being discussed she would not tolerate foolish remarks, and her reaction tended to be swift and to the point!

Although Genet felt that her parents were genuinely fond of each other, over the years the relationship deteriorated and their endless bickering began to affect the children; so at an early age she decided to take the daring step of moving out. As soon as she had completed seventh grade in Mendefera, her hometown, she took sewing classes and began to make dresses for her mother, her sisters, and even for friends and neighbors free of charge. Strong-willed by nature, she resisted the traditional arranged marriage.

After acquiring some skill as a dressmaker, Genet moved to Asmara and began a new life for herself. She rented two rooms, using one as her sewing room. The business boomed. Her two sisters came to town and joined her. It was the custom in many Eritrean families that the first-born take some of the responsibility for raising and educating the younger siblings, and Genet was no exception.

When her two sisters came to Asmara to attend school away from their quarrelling parents, Genet rented a three-room house with a kitchen and a bathroom. She was not only interested in making a living; she loved to see well-dressed women and girls, and she did her job with passion and skill. Her reputation as a dressmaker spread and she imagined herself one day opening a shop in the center of Asmara, separate from her home. Such were Genet's aspirations when she became active in the underground movement and joined a cell of the EPLF.

Then, in the middle of one night, she and her sisters heard heavy footsteps followed by banging on their door. Genet had the presence of mind to tell her sisters to slip through the window and into the house next door: She and her neighbor had prepared this escape plan that was all too common in Asmara at that time.

One of the sisters made it, but it was too late for fifteen-year-old Teka.

The soldiers did not wait to be admitted — they broke in. Teka was frightened and began to cry. The soldiers dragged both girls out of the house, beating them with the muzzles of their guns, and threw them into the back seat of a Land Rover. They had to sit in the car for two hours while their house was being searched. When the soldiers were finally ready to drive off, it was nearly dawn and the stars were fast disappearing from the sky. The city was lifeless except for the hum of the Land Rover and the barking of dogs.

The two girls were taken to Kagnew Station, the former United States communications base that had been taken over by the Ethiopian army. Inside the base, they were made to wait some three hours outside the prison buildings. Then two soldiers appeared, and between them walked a hooded man. One of the soldiers asked: "Is she the one?" Just as he replied "yes," the hood fell from the man's face and Genet recognized him instantly.

The sisters were taken to separate rooms for interrogation.

"Girl," began Genet's interrogator, "Askale, your collaborator, has come to his senses. He is now ready to serve mother Ethiopia and to fully cooperate. He will be a free man as soon as he has participated in a rehabilitation program for a few weeks. He told us about your activities. Not only are you a member of an underground cell but you have direct connection with the *shiftas* in the field. You look young and innocent, but we happen to know that you are one of their main informers. Now tell us everything. If you try to deny even the smallest shred of information, you will be leaving this room minus your head."

Genet's ear was hurting from the forceful blow one of the soldiers had delivered while she was trying to board the Land Rover, but she gathered her strength and replied:

"I knew this man as a door-to-door coal vendor. Whenever I bought coal from him, I offered him a cup of tea — that is the custom. But I have never had any connection with the *tegadelti*."

"How about the money and the revolver we found in your house, that Askale showed us?" the interrogator continued.

"I'm a dressmaker, and certainly I keep some cash. As for any revolver... considering how evil he is, I would not be surprised if he put it there himself. I don't know why he chose to pick on me."

The interrogator took Genet to another room and stuffed a vomit-stained wad of cloth in her mouth. He beat her for what seemed like three hours all over her body, especially her back and her abdomen, but most particularly the soles of her feet. Genet saw that the interrogator's hands were raw from beating her.

Although she was petite, Genet's inner strength was fierce, and she survived the torture. For the first ten days that she was held in solitary confinement at Kagnew Station, she refused to eat the food they brought her; there were no lunch parcels for the two sisters from the outside, for nobody knew where to find them. After the tenth day she felt so weak that she forced herself to eat some of the food that the guards brought her.

Genet was kept in solitary confinement at Kagnew Station for a whole month and was interrogated and beaten twice after the initial session. Then she was transferred to the Palace Prison. Her youngest sister, meanwhile, who had not been involved in any underground activities, was beaten mildly and released.

Genet looked like a walking corpse when she was transferred to the *ghebi*. After two weeks, she was moved once more, this time to Haz Haz Prison to await trial; she had had one hearing at military court when I joined them. She never seemed to worry about losing her hearing in her right ear — which seemed highly probable to us — and she never wished to discuss the possibility of being unable to bear a child because of her internal injuries.

Genet was a young woman of incredible courage.

# Nine

"Prisoner Abeba," called one of the guards.

What! I said to myself. I was told there would be no interrogation at Haz Haz. My God, am I not through with it!

But the guard saw my apprehension and told me there were visitors to see me.

Relief!

It was only when she went to the Palace Prison to deliver my lunch that my mother discovered I had been transferred. Two hours after my arrival at Haz Haz Prison there she was, along with Mesfun and my father.

Slowly I walked through the long corridor to the door; I couldn't believe my eyes when I saw my parents and my husband, from a distance, behind barbed wire. I wanted to embrace them, but we were not permitted to get that close.

Mother wept openly. Mesfun and *Abboi* acted brave and tried to make me feel comfortable. After some time I was ordered back inside, and it was only when the three of them turned to leave that I, too, felt the emotion welling up inside me. All three of them came again the next day, with food, pillows, a mattress, and a Bible. We felt a little more relaxed this time, and my mother and I were able to talk.

In the hope that my release was imminent, Mesfun and I thought it would be better if the children waited until I got home rather than see me behind bars. But after three weeks of waiting and waiting, we decided they should come to the prison.

It was therefore arranged that on the third Saturday after my transfer, the four of them would visit me in Haz Haz. On the morning of the big day, I woke up disoriented but happy. I had dreamt that I was holding my daughters close and telling them we would never again be separated. When my mind cleared and I realized it was a dream, I panicked. I was afraid I would break down in front of my children, that I would be unable to hold back my tears.

Even though my stomach was in knots, I made myself as presentable as possible. Since mirrors were not permitted, I had to rely on the judgment of my cellmates. They all assured me that I looked fine, yet somehow their faces told me they could clearly see the anxiety that I was trying so desperately to conceal.

I was the first prisoner called to see her visitors that Saturday. With my chin up, and with a forced smile, I walked down the corridor and came to a stop one foot away from the door.

There, standing face to face with me, behind barbed wire, were my four children.

Ruth had never worn a *netsela* before, but I noticed that she had one on now, and she looked very graceful in it. Tamar's long hair was cut short and she wore a short skirt. Muzit and Senait had on cute dresses and wore their hair in their usual pony tails.

I tried to comment on how wonderful they looked — but my speech was incoherent. The fact that I could not get closer and embrace them made it all the more painful, and I had to battle with myself to keep calm. When my husband saw me struggling, he went to the office of the chief guard to ask if the girls could come inside with me for a brief reunion. The chief guard came to survey the situation. When he saw the children weeping and me standing there motionless, he said that my two younger daughters would be allowed to come inside.

After some moments of total silence, I opened my mouth to speak: "Please let my other children come in too," I pleaded.

"For security reasons, I cannot let your grown-up daughters in. Proceed to the office and you will meet the younger two," he ordered.

I avoided the eyes of Ruth and Tamar and was led to the office, about twenty-five yards away, where a woman motioned for me to take a seat on one of the four chairs.

I had barely sat down when in walked another guard with Muzit and Senait. I stood immediately and they threw themselves at me, their tears brushing my face. Stroking their hair gently and kissing them all over their faces and hands, I felt that at least half of my world was secure. Then I tried to be cheerful and act as though everything was completely normal.

"Mommy, how long are you going to stay here?" Muzit asked.

"I don't know yet — not too long, I hope."

"Can we see your room, where you sleep?" Senait joined in.

"The prison rules don't allow for visitors to go into the bedrooms, even children like you. But we all have good beds and nice bedside tables and everything. We live very well here." I could see from their faces that their suspicions had not been allayed.

Although I had managed to keep the tears from flowing up to that point, the emotional upheaval was bound to manifest itself in some way, and now my legs shook so violently that I had to take the children off my lap. I saw that one of the guards was weeping, while the other three were simply looking down at the floor.

The guard told me with tears in her eyes that it was time for Muzit and Senait to go and for me to return to my cell. With some degree of outward calm, I told my babies that we would be seeing each other more often from then on, and that I had some great stories from my cellmates to tell them when I was released. Again, they demanded to know when I was coming home.

"I don't know; it may not be too long. Just keep on hoping and praying," I said.

Muzit told me that her teacher at the Comboni School was praying for me, and then with a final big hug we parted.

It was becoming impossible to hold back the tears, so I dared not even look at my family beyond the fence on the way back to the cell. Again, I avoided looking Ruth and Tamar in the eye.

Ignoring my cellmates, who were so anxious to hear about the reunion, I let all my anguish explode. I wiped away the tears and felt a great sense of relief. The ordeal of facing my children after twelve weeks in detention was over, and something inside me assured me that things were going to be better from then on.

The children kept coming every Sunday, and their second visit was not as painful as the first. The authorities never again allowed Muzit and Senait to come inside, though. Seeing them over the fence, nonetheless, well dressed and looking pretty, telling me about their school and about the stream of visitors who kept bringing them treats — it was my greatest source of comfort during those trying weeks at Haz Haz Prison.

The night after my daughters' second visit, Berekti read us some verses from the Bible and we all said good night. The lights were never turned out at Haz Haz Prison.

I could not sleep that particular night, not even a wink. I felt hot and my palms were sweaty. It was a good time to reflect. Since there was far less tension at Haz Haz Prison than there had been at the wretched Palace, one could think about things other than merely surviving the torture and the interrogation. My mind wandered far and wide.

The EPLF — once it has succeeded in liberating the country, what does it stand for, and what does it mean to me personally and to my family? I posed the question to myself. I thought of the principles laid down by the EPLF. Thanks to my parents, I had had a fairly good education. Thanks to Mesfun, our children went to the best school, even though we sometimes worried that they would end up alienated from their own culture. With all these privileges, why was I not happy and at peace?

No person and no family exists in isolation. No conscious, aware person could be content living in our country as it was. I was affected by the sight of Eritrean children in tatters, eating scraps of rotting fruit in the market. The heartbreaking stories of my *ghebi* and Haz Haz cellmates were, in fact, perfect examples of the sorry, unjust lot of most Eritreans.

The EPLF's values seemed to offer the changes that I craved: pride in being Eritrean and African; free education for all children — urban and rural alike — up to the twelfth grade, combining theory with practice; the creation of job opportunities; women's rights, including equal pay for work of equal value; economic development; and freedom of speech and assembly, freedom from fear and want, freedom to breathe the beautiful and healthy air of Eritrea.

Critics in the West called the EPLF Marxists or socialists. Marxist or not, their statement of principles appealed to me, and in the deepest recesses of my heart I hoped that in their ambitious push towards economic prosperity they would not make the mistake of losing touch with individuals, families, and humanity; that they would understand that development follows only when minds and hearts are free; that love and honesty are far more powerful than fear and corruption.

Toward dawn I was worn out from turning these thoughts over and over in my mind all night long, and I wanted to doze off. But I was afraid I would miss Mesfun's visit in the morning. Throughout my stay at Haz Haz, he came every single morning between a quarter to eight and a quarter past eight, and Mother came between one and two o'clock every afternoon.

In my state of exhaustion I hated the idea of seeing Mesfun through the barbed wire. I wanted to be in his bosom. I saw him in the flesh every day, right in front of me, yet I could not touch him.

I hated prison.

# Ten

After a one-month stay in Haz Haz Prison, I was transported by Volkswagen to Kagnew Station for trial in a military court. Our car approached the gate behind an open truck full of male prisoners. When it was our turn, the driver presented his identification papers and the two armed guards beside me leaned forward to show their faces.

"Who is she?" asked the short, dark-skinned checkpoint guard.

"Prisoner, of course..." replied our driver.

"Oh, one of the *shifta* women. Damn them. Go on in."

It was quite a contrast from the days when Mesfun and I would go through these same gates and a casual American GI would give us a smile, salute, and respectfully tell us to proceed. The once pristine Kagnew communications base was now full of irritated, ugly voices; the ground was littered with paper, and armored cars and armed men were everywhere. Not only were prisoners housed here, it was the headquarters from which the Ethiopian generals ordered the destruction of our homes and the liquidation of our people.

The truckload of male prisoners and our Volkswagen both pulled up in front of a once-beautiful barrack with a manicured lawn that might have originally been used as a U.S. officers' residence. Now it was surrounded by patches of dry grass and a few miserable-looking weeds. This was the military court.

The prisoners jumped from their truck one by one under heavy guard; two of them were in chains. The Volkswagen and the truck roared away, and we prisoners were ordered to form two lines along the wall of the building opposite the court. The male inmates were from Sembel Prison and they numbered twenty-seven in all. I was the only woman.

"Talking among prisoners is forbidden. Do you understand?" shouted a soldier who came out of the courthouse. He told our guards to watch us closely.

Standing in the open air under a vast, clear sky with my fellow prisoners made me tolerate anything at that point, even the crude orders of ignorant bullies.

Between nine a.m. and noon, only three prisoners were called for trial, and then I was the fourth. As I walked in between two guards, I felt myself being carefully observed by the three judges who were wearing army and air force uniforms. The small courtroom had two large windows and there were men scattered about the five rows of benches. The government had provided me with a lawyer, and of course, the all-important prosecutor was there. My two guards backed away and I was told to remain standing on the prisoner's stand. The prosecutor read two pages of accusations against me and I was asked if these were true.

"Not true," I answered.

"How can you deny it when we have proof that you actually served the so-called EPLF in many ways, from collecting money from businessmen to redirecting public relief money?"

"Because I did not," I replied.

My lawyer then intervened. He said that there was insufficient evidence for these charges and that I had done nothing wrong as far as he could determine. My case was therefore postponed until the next hearing; it had not lasted long at all. I stepped down from the stand and joined the other prisoners outside the building.

By one o'clock the guards were tired and had lost interest in keeping watch over our every movement. A high school classmate of my brother Solomon, who was being held in the Palace Prison and was also standing in line, managed to send me a note. When I later opened it in Haz Haz, all it said was: "Because you are Solomon's sister, you are my sister too. Please pray for me. I think they are going to kill me." He had a very rough time at *ghebi*, and would be terrified every time he was called for interrogation. He would send similar notes to me on two further occasions.

The court was adjourned for the day by half past two, and the Volkswagen came to take me back to my cellmates.

Through friends in Addis Ababa, Mesfun found out that there were political differences between the three judges and the governor, General Getachow Nadow; and that, in fact, the judges held the General in some contempt because of his crude methods and his pretentiousness. Mesfun decided to make use of this information, to exploit to the fullest the rift between the two camps. He even managed to talk his way into the court for my trial. The main concern of the judges, became proving that Getachow Nadow was wrong, and discrediting him. The prosecutor, moreover, did not have enough evidence to convict me, and after three hearings I was acquitted. Mesfun was in the courtroom when the acquittal was pronounced and our eyes met.

But as I moved away from the stand a uniformed man came up and said that I would be going back to the Palace until a special order came from General Getachow Nadow. Mesfun and I were both struck numb.

Every time I went to trial, my family firmly believed I would be set free. The day of my last trial, our kitchen and bedroom were painted, my favorite tablecloths were taken out, the houseplants were meticulously cleaned leaf by leaf, and flowers were placed in every room of the house.

My cellmates, who also had high hopes that I was going to be released, prepared their oral messages and their carefully-worded notes to loved ones. Then word came that despite my acquittal I had been sent back to the Palace Prison.

"What! Does she have a second charge?" gasped Genet. Fana feared that she might be given a longer sentence than she had anticipated. Saba was despondent. "What is going on here? Have you forsaken us, Lord?" murmured Sister Weini. Despair crept into the hearts of those who had expected to be freed.

Mesfun had to face our daughters without their mother. My father and mother and all our relatives were in our house awaiting my return.

"Wherever she may be, protect her, Oh Lord," *Abboi* said. *Addei* simply kept silent. While Ruth played the protective older sister, Tamar and Muzit wept. Senait somehow believed I had merely been delayed a while.

My family picked up my belongings from Haz Haz and sent them to the *ghebi* prison. The cells were packed with new faces. There remained only one cell for women, and Ribka and Tsegga were two of its five occupants. I found Ribka to be dreadfully depressed.

"This place is only supposed to be for short stays," she lamented. "Everybody else has gone off to Haz Haz, but there's no hope for us. Those bastards. Why didn't the sons of bitches just finish us off?"

I was alarmed."My God, Ribka. What is happening to you?" I asked.

"Can't you see?" Ribka raised her voice. "My faith is getting weaker by the day. I don't even know if I believe in God any more.... I'm so scared."

My heart went out to her. I was so glad to be back with Ribka, a girl whose friendship I shall cherish forever. We prayed night after night and we talked endlessly.

I found Tsegga downhearted as well, but she did not seem to have given up the way Ribka had. Her mother in Italy had heard of her imprisonment at long last. Now her worries were centered on her mother's reaction to the bad news.

So returning to that hellish prison after my acquittal was not as terrible as it could have been. At least I had my health this time around, I told myself. It occurred to me to send a request to the head of the prison, the Major, asking that I be allowed to clean the toilets that had just recently been installed inside our building. The Major responded by coming to the cell and greeting me—after all, I was acquitted by the law. He said I was welcome to clean as much as I wanted. There were no cleaning materials, however—I had to ask my family to provide me with some.

I would get up at about half past six, and then at seven o'clock my cellmates and I would go to the outside toilet before eating a bite of breakfast. At about nine o'clock, with great enthusiasm, I would begin cleaning the toilets. Then I would sweep and mop the corridor, and this would take approximately two and a half hours. It was an excellent way to get some exercise. After four days, they allowed me to help deliver food parcels to the inmates and to collect the empty containers. I enjoyed the chance to exchange a few words with my fellow prisoners while handing them their lunches; but I was never asked to take notes back and forth, as a fellow prisoner had once gladly done for Mesfun and I.

As compensation for all my work, I was granted permission to stay outside in the sun for half an hour during the afternoons.

After two weeks of this I was again sent back to Haz Haz, where I would stay for another six weeks. Shuttling between these two prisons became routine for me.

During those last six weeks at Haz Haz, there occurred an event well worth relating. A child was born to an inmate.

Hiwot was only two months pregnant when she was first detained. Her fiancé was an active underground member of the EPLF in Asmara. The secret police had nabbed him in a tea shop, and his whereabouts were unknown. It was rumored that he had become one of Colonel Zenebe Asfaw's victims at the notorious Expo Prison.

Nineteen years old and a high school dropout, Hiwot had been an inmate of the Palace Prison for four months before I had first set foot there. It was a miracle that the poor girl did not miscarry during her interrogation. She was subjected to the sadistic numbers eight and nine torture techniques, placed upside down and beaten on the soles of her feet and on her back. They also stomped on her abdomen, as if they knew that life was beginning there. Yet the torture did not embitter Hiwot, nor did she seem to regret having become pregnant.

I noticed that Hiwot's frustration only really began when she could no longer hide her pregnancy from her mother, who would visit three or four times each week. Hiwot created excuses for not stepping out of the prison door to see her mother. Twice she had the guards say that she was not feeling well. When the worried woman pleaded to be told the truth about her daughter, one of the Eritrean guards finally gave in and told her that Hiwot was pregnant and that she was ashamed to face her mother.

"If her father was alive, she would never have done this," was the mother's response. "Does this mean that all the years I labored to raise her properly were in vain?" She was inconsolable. Hiwot's mother seemed to take the news of her daughter's pregnancy harder than her imprisonment!

After the initial shock, however, mother and daughter had no choice but to stand face-to-face one Saturday morning, separated by the barbed wire. Both women were in tears that memorable day. "I didn't mean to hurt you, Mother. I didn't mean it," sobbed Hiwot. "Forget about my dreams and my pride," countered her mother. "If you could only get out of here and deliver the baby at home, I would consider myself lucky."

Hiwot impressed her cellmates as a childish and naive girl, but I discovered that this was not her character at all. One morning when we were all out in the prison yard, I happened to be standing near Hiwot. The sun was beating down and both of us were tired, so we went back inside and sat on a folded blanket in our room.

"Mother worked hard and sacrificed to raise me and my two younger sisters," said Hiwot, her childlike expression fading as we talked. Her mother had made a good living for her family from her small business, she told me, but a year before the fighting broke out in Asmara the business started falling. Hiwot saw her mother worrying, and she decided to drop out of ninth grade and look for a job. She even applied for factory work that required no education, but without luck.

While she was job-hunting, Hiwot met Kiflom, a twenty-five-year-old teacher. He encouraged her to continue reading books. As the days went by, they became close friends and he convinced her to join the underground EPLF cell of which he was a leader.

"He really is a diehard nationalist. You know, it was Kiflom who made me see that it was not the Ethiopian people as such who are our enemies, but the Ethiopian government," said Hiwot. The friendship grew into something more; much as she loved him, however, Hiwot was not ready to accept Kiflom's engagement ring. When I asked her why, she replied: "I still hoped to find a job and help my mother first."

One day, Kiflom and Hiwot went to Bet Gherghis woods, about one mile from Asmara on the way to Massawa, to get away from the constant tension of the city.

"As we walked deeper and deeper into the woods, we were awed by the total silence. We sat under a big tree to listen to the singing of the birds and the rustling of the leaves. Then we started listening to each other's heartbeat... it all happened that day," Hiwot sighed. Three weeks later Kiflom was snatched from her. Hiwot had no illusions. She knew that there was a distinct possibility that Kiflom had been killed. But she had to be strong in order to carry the baby to term.

"My mother and the rest of my family... and all of you too.... You may think my child will be born out of wedlock," she said, oblivious to the inmates who came and went during our conversation, "but it is just not true. In my heart I am married to Kiflom. Heaven, the trees, the birds, nature, are my witness. I've known no man but him. It was in honor of Kiflom that I bore three straight days of torture at the *ghebi* prison without making a sound."

I was in a trance when Hiwot finished telling me her story. The nineteen-year-old girl had a heavy burden to carry. Hiwot's labour pains began in the evening and kept her awake the whole night. The next morning, she was sent to the Itegue Menen Hospital, under heavy guard, and there she gave birth to a baby girl. Hiwot's mother, sadly, was not allowed to hold her first grandchild. Hiwot's father had died when she was five years old, and here was his grandchild born in prison and orphaned from birth. It was later confirmed that Kiflom had been murdered.

Mother and baby came back to Haz Haz two days after the birth. Sad as it was to see a child born in prison, our newborn inmate brought life to all of us: We took turns holding her and taking care of her. She brought back to me the joyful memory of the birth of my daughters.

# Eleven

In 1965, the Association of American Women in Asmara, which counted among its members the wives of diplomats and United States Information Service (USIS) personnel, invited a group of Eritrean women to a get-together at the residence of the consul general. Since my husband worked at the consulate, I was one of those invited. The event was deemed a success, and three more social and cultural-exchange gatherings followed, each held at the home of a different woman. As far as I could see, it was pointless to continue meeting just for the purpose of socializing. So at the next event I suggested that we take advantage of the meeting to do something worthwhile for other women. Many of the participants took to this idea at once, and several of us then met to discuss how we would proceed.

As Mesfun was heavily involved in the activities of the YMCA, he encouraged us to develop the idea of a sister organization. A wider group of women, gave their wholehearted support to the plan. After we had received advice from the secretary of the YMCA, the late Teklehaimant Mengesteab, and the participation of Eva Kelly, the wife of one of the U.S. vice-consuls, a local YWCA was established in Asmara.

In a third world country like Eritrea, and in a small city like Asmara, where there existed no other organization serving the interests of women and girls, the YWCA served many. It conducted language classes in Italian and English, and it offered courses in literacy, cooking, housekeeping, dressmaking, first aid, child care, bookkeeping, and financial management. Y-Teen clubs were organized in secondary schools. Teenagers used the playgrounds for basketball, tennis, and volleyball. There were educational lectures by a wide variety of speakers. With the exception of three paid employees, all the services were carried out by volunteers.

The Asmara YWCA, where I served as a chairperson for the first two terms, was created in 1965 and closed down by the Dergue in 1980. I would be doing the organization a disservice by trying to squeeze its history into these few paragraphs, but suffice it to say that the YWCA played a vital role in the community. The only reason I mention it here is because it spawned the relief association that would have some connection with my detention.

The YWCA did what it could with its meager resources, but as the years rolled by we found that we were not able to reach those girls and women who needed our help the most. This would require resources and commitment from the wider community as well as the government, for the sad reality is that in our part of the world, the government has to be with you in order not to be against you.

One Sunday in early November 1973, Mesfun and I were taking the children to the garden of the municipal dam at Mainefhi, three miles from Asmara on the road to Keren. We were about to make a turn in the road, when I saw a pregnant woman with a baby on her back, holding a child of about four by the hand and balancing a small sack of grain on her head. The limbs of the four-year-old were like sticks and he had to struggle to keep up with his mother. The woman was trying to cross the road and we slowed down to let her pass.

Suddenly our eyes met and something touched my heart; I felt so much compassion for this woman. When we got home, I sat alone for some time and thought about her and her unfortunate children. Why am I so disturbed? I asked myself. After all, I had grown up in a neighborhood where such scenes were not unusual. But the expression on the woman's face had touched me. It was not only that she was pregnant, and carried a child on her back and a sack on her head, and dragged another child along by the hand; it was her expression of hunger and despair that struck me. Going back over the years, I came to the realization that there had always been a lack of protein in the diet of our people. How could one expect otherwise after years of colonization and subjugation?

I began to more consciously observe people every day,

especially in the local market where villagers would come to sell the produce from their farms and to buy consumer goods. I detected hunger in many faces, and I tossed and turned in my bed every night.

I also learned that the drought was more severe than people had perceived it to be. My encounter with the woman on the road to Keren occurred a year after the Ethiopian famine had been in the news everywhere, particularly the bloated bellies and the hauntingly mournful eyes in Wollo and Tigrai provinces. The British journalist Jonathan Dimbleby had brought the tragedy to the attention of the world, despite the crude conspiracy of Haile Selassie and his government to keep it a secret. Indeed, it was very hard for me, to conceive of the fact that people were actually dying of hunger not only in Ethiopia, but also in Eritrea.

A Canadian missionary from the Sudan Interior Mission, a close friend of the family, came to my office to see me. His mission had started a program to help the starving in Tigrai. "Is it really true?" I asked him. "Are people really going without enough food to keep the body and soul together?"

"Yes, it is true." The missionary recounted the classic human tragedy: children suckling the breasts of their dead mothers; families too weak to bury their dead; people walking miles in search of food and water only to die within a few feet of the shelters erected by the international aid organisations.

I volunteered to go to Tigrai during my annual vacation and help in whatever way I could, but the missionary thought the situation would be too much for me to bear. Besides, he said, what was needed most was medical help. In fact, a close friend, Mulunesh Woldegiorgis, an Eritrean nurse and midwife with whom I had worked at the YWCA and who had later been transferred to Addis Ababa, had already been to Wollo. She had convinced eight of her students to go along as well, and they put in eighteen hours a day for a month. Mulunesh took this courageous decision before the Ethiopian government had even admitted that the famine existed; she risked losing her job and could have run into serious trouble with the authorities. I would hear of her heroic stand only much later.

"If there is anything you and Mesfun can do, I will let you know," said the missionary, smiling wanly as we shook hands. He turned and began to walk away, slowly, as though he carried the weight of the world on his shoulders. Then he turned back to me and shook his head. "This is a moral failure on the part of not only the Ethiopian government, but all humanity," he added as he left my office.

The long war and the drought had touched just about every person in Eritrea, and we were by now all too aware of the awful hunger that was killing scores of innocent people in various regions of Ethiopia. Yet I had never imagined that people were actually perishing of starvation in Eritrea. The sight of that mother I encountered on the road, however, made it clear to me that as hunger progresses the end result is death, and that many of my own people were not far from it.

Death by starvation was something my mind could not grasp. I began to lose more and more sleep and to have nightmares night after night, and the pounds seemed to fall away from my body for lack of an appetite. Finally, I shared my concerns with close friends at the YWCA. We set up an informal meeting of the YWCA board to discuss the problem. One of the board members told us about a relative who came from his village to seek her help. The family was living on just one meal every two days. The mother was eating virtually nothing.

Finally, it was decided that we would conduct preliminary research into exactly what parts of Eritrea were most affected by the drought. We were aware, of course, that the prime cause of the hunger was the Ethiopian aggression; but at this initial stage we were careful to avoid even the words "war" and "fighting." After the first month we had gathered enough statistical data to prepare a comprehensive paper on the subject. Then as mothers, we felt it was our solemn duty to bring the situation to the attention of the government, whether or not it had thus far intentionally ignored it.

We requested a meeting with the governor of Eritrea, Debebe Hailemariam, to inform him of our findings. The world had condemned the Emperor and his government for attempting to conceal the famine in his own country; and we reasoned that although they could care less about what happened to the Eritreans, they might very well be concerned about international opinion should the same catastrophe befall Eritrea.

Our speculations were accurate. The governor listened to the three of us attentively, said that he appreciated our maternal concern, and granted us permission to form a committee from the community to address the matter of the famine.

The YWCA called together a meeting of government officials, representatives from churches and mosques, and business and community leaders. We presented our findings and announced that the government had given us the green light to form a committee. The representative from the Catholic Church, Padre Angelico, was particularly delighted that the government had given its approval, for his church had been helping the needy in the surrounding villages and had feared that they would be stopped. Now they would be able to continue their work through the new committee.

Thus was born the Relief and Rehabilitation Association for Eritrea, the first of its kind in Eritrea. The YWCA had become the proud mother of a worthy humanitarian organisation.

The board members of the new Association were not only committed but knowledgeable. The main office was in Asmara and branches were established in each of the nine provinces. A fund-raising committee was also set up in Addis Ababa. The Association had seven paid employees and hundreds of volunteers. The name itself and its mandate touched the hearts of Eritreans, and thousands of people rallied to the cause. I remember an elderly woman coming to the office and donating fifty of the two hundred and fifty dollars her son had sent her from Sweden. Consular missions, businesses, service organizations such as the Rotary and Lion's Clubs, the Catholic Church — all gave moral support as well as handsome financial contributions.

It is not my intention here to provide a detailed history of the Relief and Rehabilitation Association for Eritrea and what it did during the eight short months of its existence. I present this brief history only because it had a bearing on my six months' imprisonment.

In any case, after the initial relief campaign, the Red Sea branch advanced from a program of immediate relief to one of rehabilitation, and they requested seeds and tractors to help needy farmers. The request was granted by the board in Asmara.

The Ethiopian government was rumoured to be preparing a take-over of the Association. It felt threatened by the spirit of cooperation and self-help among the recipients of relief, the dedication of the Association's workers and volunteers, and — perhaps most worrisome of all — the spirit of unity engendered throughout the general public.

The rumour that the Dergue might take over the Association reached the ears of the EPLF, and it prompted them to seize the three tractors to use them in agricultural development in the liberated areas.

The government accused the secretary and the treasurer of the Red Sea branch of being accomplices in the seizure of the tractors, and they were imprisoned. (Much later, as an inmate, I would become panic-stricken upon catching a glimpse of Dr. Assefaw Tekeste, chair of the Red Sea branch, on the steps of the Major's office in the Palace Prison.)

When news of the arrests reached me, as chair of the Association, I felt it was my duty to immediately appeal to the governor, General Getachow Nadow.

Getting an appointment was not difficult at all. But when I was shown into the governor's office, perhaps I failed to bow as low as I was expected to in Ethiopian tradition — that was one thing I could never do. When Emperor Haile Selassie had come to Asmara and paid a visit to the YWCA in 1972, as president and host I was told by the protocol people how to curtsy. I could not bring myself then to bow any lower than I normally would for any elderly person, and I would not do so now. That was one mark against me. The second *faux pas* occurred when I declined the General's offer of tea — graciously, I thought; he ordered for both of us, nonetheless, and I left mine untouched, not being much of a tea drinker.

"What were the circumstances behind the rebels stealing the tractors?" he asked abruptly, placing his half-empty cup in the saucer and looking angry.

"I have no idea what the circumstances were, and neither does the chair of the Massawa branch," I replied. "What I do know is that two of our branch officers are in Massawa Prison."

"So what do you want me to do about it?" asked the governor with a shrug of his shoulders and just a trace of a sneer. "If they have collaborated with the shiftas, surely they deserve at least this."

"General..." I tried to keep my composure. "These are peaceable men whose sole aim is to help the needy women and children of the motherland."

"Which motherland?" he shot back.

I had been caught off-guard.

"You are joking, General. There is only one motherland — Ethiopia." Anything less would have amounted to digging my own grave.

The governor's face turned cold, and I knew that I had not fooled him.

"I will see to it that their case is investigated. If they are as innocent as you claim, they will be released." The governor stood, signalling the end of the meeting. Then suddenly he said: "If it was not for the rebels — your brothers — Ethiopia would have concentrated on economic development. Now that they have taken the tractors, I hope people will understand that the EPLF, or ELF, or whatever it is they call themselves, are not for helping their fellow Eritreans, as they claim to be."

I did not know how to reply to that.

The governor courteously shook hands as I took my leave, but it must have been during this one-hour meeting that he perceived me to be an enemy of the Dergue. When I was later arrested by the *afagn*, he sent an order to the Major at the *ghebi* prison to be especially harsh with me.

"I cannot detain this woman indefinitely," the General confided to a friend, (as it was told to us much later by an insider). "I am being pressured from all sides — even the churches are behind her. But we must find some evidence to prosecute her; she is not only a collaborator, but a rebel herself."

That explains why the General had me sent back to the Palace Prison even after I had been acquitted by the court.

Just as the rumor had predicted, a government representative convened a sudden meeting of the board of directors of the Relief and Rehabilitation Association for Eritrea and ordered all of our assets transferred to the government coffers. This included a half million dollars earmarked for various rehabilitation and development projects. Our Association was terminated.

After the government took over in November 1974, they did not continue relief activities in Eritrea, as they had promised us they would. Instead, they escalated their military operations, thereby rendering the situation much more desperate.

Four months after the closing of the Association, Padre Angelico summoned church and mosque leaders as well as other key citizens of Asmara to a meeting with the idea of forming a new committee, the Religious Relief Service. Padre Angelico was named chair. He was aware of no rule, said Padre Angelico, that prevented the dispensing of aid from the premises of mosques or churches. The Religious Relief Service therefore proceeded to deliver food to the destitute and to displaced persons from the surrounding villages.

This practice continued for three months without the knowledge of the Dergue. But when the government found out about the new system, they ordered an immediate halt to the distribution of grain and powdered milk.

#  Twelve

In the late afternoon of the thirtieth of March 1976, a guard came rushing to our room and with a smile ordered me to pack up immediately.

"Why? Where am I going?"

"Maybe you are going to be released. I don't know. Just hurry," she replied.

It did not take me long to prepare my bundle.

"Long live our *tegadelti*, and don't forget us," pleaded Genet as we embraced for the last time. Sister Weini hugged me tightly. "May you have a fulfilling life, and may God help our sons and daughters to be masters of their own land," she said, her hands outstretched. Fana, Saba, and Berekti just wept as I hugged and squeezed them all.

The guard returned and I could tell from her stern expression that she was not going to let me say my goodbyes to the other prisoners individually, so I just waved to them all.

"I hope and pray you will never be back here," said the guard, an Eritrean woman, as she led me down the corridor to the office. I realized then that she had been rushing me only because she wanted to get me out of there as quickly as possible.

The way the head of Haz Haz Prison greeted me when we arrived at his office, was a clear indication that indeed I was going to be released. He stood and shook my hand as though I were an important visitor.

"I am handing you over to these people," he said, looking in the direction of two armed guards. "I won't be seeing you any more. Goodbye and good luck."

My bundle was searched; luckily, the letters that Mesfun had smuggled to me were well hidden. We boarded a jeep, and as soon as the driver started it up, I asked where they were taking me.

"The *ghebi* prison. That is where you're being released from," answered one of my escorts.

Although the Dergue were committing horrendous crimes against Eritreans every day, and one learned to expect anything, it had been hard for my family to comprehend the cruelty of detaining me after I had been acquitted by a military court. General Getachow Nadow himself admitted that there was so much pressure from so many quarters that he had no choice but to release me.

But "release" in this case did not mean that I would be free to go home and be with my family. It meant that I would be exiled to Addis Ababa, and it was made very clear to me that I could never again set foot in Eritrea as long as Getachow Nadow remained governor.

I was hardly enthusiastic when I received this news from the head of the Palace Prison, the Major; but anything would be preferable to staying behind bars.

"Thank you, Major. When am I going to Addis?" I inquired.

"If there was a flight tonight, you could go right away. But you'll have to wait until tomorrow. Your office has been told to reserve you a seat. And your family has been informed; they are bringing you some clothing now."

What a contrast between the way the Major treated me during my interrogation and on the eve of my release!

"Can I spend the night with my children, Major?"

"I'm afraid not. The instructions from the governor are to fly you direct to Addis. I have to abide by his orders."

Mesfun had been defiant during his interrogation and throughout his stay in prison, and the Major did not want to see him again, so my father brought me my clothes. It was so wonderful to see him at the Palace not as an inmate but as a free man.

"Special favour for you, lady," said the Major as I was about to be escorted to the cell for the night. "Your relatives can come to the airport to see you off tomorrow. Your father has been informed accordingly."

At *ghebi*, I found my old cellmate and friend Ribka in much better spirits this time, and we talked the whole night, without catching a wink of sleep, while Tsegga and our other two cellmates slept around midnight.

I left the Palace Prison on the thirty-first of March 1976, at seven o'clock in the morning. The black iron gates closed behind the Land Rover and we set out for the airport, with me sitting between an armed guard and the driver. The city was ominously quiet at that hour; there was no traffic except for a few military vehicles, and the only sign of human life were odd soldiers here and there, guarding key buildings.

I was looking forward to seeing my children and my family, and I was very excited. When we passed the Expo site, nevertheless, I could not help but shudder. Everything I had heard from Ribka, an eyewitness to the horrors, came to mind, and the joy of being released paled for a moment.

As we approached the airport, the driver slowed down and I spotted a large crowd just outside the entrance. It was my family and friends.

As I stepped out of the Land Rover, still under escort, Mesfun's aunt handed Senait to me. I could not say a word. As I was about to gather her into my arms Muzit was pushed toward me and I found it impossible to hold both of them. Moreover, Ruth and Tamar were all over me.

My guard wanted me to check in, so I had to cut short my visit with my children, my parents, my sister, my brothers, and all the friends and relatives who had come to see me off. There was just enough time to greet everybody briefly before the guard escorted me to the ramp. I thanked him for his patience, waved to everyone for the last time, and boarded the plane.

As we left the ground and flew high above the clouds, I was euphoric. Of the countless flights I had taken during the course of my life, this was the best.

Many people met me at the airport in Addis Ababa. By that time, several hundred Eritreans had been forced, either directly or indirectly, to leave Eritrea and settle in Addis. I was fortunate enough to be put up at the home of a childhood friend who worked for the Economic Commission for Africa, the late Alganesh Gebremariam; her family gave me red carpet treatment.

Mesfun followed three days later, and we spent a spectacular week together at Sodere, a resort area far away from Addis.

Every morning and every afternoon we swam in the pool, splashing and giggling. A month later, during Easter vacation, he brought all the children along and we had a wonderful long-awaited and much dreamt about reunion.

The prison ordeal was behind me but I did not forget my cellmates or the other prisoners. They were on my mind constantly.

The Ethiopian Airlines head office was located in Addis Ababa, and three weeks after my arrival I went back to work for the company. When school closed for winter vacation, my daughters all came. Mesfun secured a position at the American embassy in Addis, and we settled down and enjoyed the hospitality of our friends for the next five months. Finally, with the assistance of my friend Abebech Gebreselassie, we were able to rent a comfortable house in a nice neighborhood and find good schools for our daughters. My parents came to see us, and we had wonderful visits from many friends and relatives.

We would never have left Asmara under normal circumstances, but relocation was the only way I could get out of prison and be reunited with my family. We led a quiet life for the next year, from March 1976 to April 1977.

There were at this time many underground movements against the Dergue in Addis Ababa, and unrest was not uncommon in Ethiopian schools. Fearing that Ruth or Tamar would get involved in these activities or become incriminated, we thought for some time about the possibility of sending them back to Asmara to live with their grandparents.

The beginning of the Red Terror in 1977 prompted us to carry out this plan without further delay.

# Thirteen

When Emperor Haile Selassie was deposed in 1974, the Ethiopian people had hoped for a peaceful solution to the long-standing "problem" of Eritrea. But this was not to be. The military junta literally stole power from the citizens of Ethiopia, and its band of thugs descended upon even its own people with a force so brutal that it surpassed that of the feared Emperor.

The reign of the Red Terror was directed mainly against suspected members or sympathizers of the clandestine opposition, the Ethiopian People's Revolutionary Party (EPRP), who were distributing anti-government literature calling for civilian rule in Addis Ababa.

During the Red Terror, which commenced in early 1977 and reached its climax in early 1978, more than thirty thousand people were executed for political reasons. In a period of just one month, the Dergue's police and army squads murdered five thousand school children and university students — this in a poor third world country whose entire student population numbered no more than thirty-six thousand in 1971. A total of thirty thousand people were imprisoned in one month alone.

Addis Ababa was divided into three hundred sub-districts, each of which had its own makeshift prison and its own armed guards prowling the streets. The sub-districts were authorized to take "revolutionary measures" whenever necessary; that is, to kill at the slightest provocation. With each sub-district assigned eight to ten policemen, this made for some three thousand authorized killers in the city of Addis Ababa alone.

School children and university students caught in the act of demonstrating were gunned down on the spot. Children who managed to escape the shooting were dragged from their hiding places — from under beds and behind dressers — and shot, along with anyone else who happened to be in the house at the time.

Between fifty and a hundred people were executed every single night in Addis. More often than not, their bodies were left lying in the streets as an example to others. In the district of Mercato, and elsewhere as well, passersby were forcibly stopped and made to look at the corpses so that they could draw the necessary conclusions. The bodies of the victims — adults and children alike — were buried in mass graves after being exposed to the hot sun for hours on end. Parents who begged to have the body of a child returned to them were charged the cost of the bullet that had taken their child's life.

A particular incident that will never be erased from my mind concerns the death of a fourteen-year-old boy. His divorced mother, with whom I worked at Ethiopian Airlines, had dedicated her life to raising her only child. As she was about to go to bed one night, there was loud banging on the door. She wondered who it could be at that hour — and whether it was the dreaded *kebeles*, the district police who had the power to imprison and murder. Before she had time to answer, the door was broken in and the half-drunk, abusive intruders demanded to know the whereabouts of her son. My co-worker was so numb with fear she could not speak. They searched the four-room house and found the boy, who woke screaming at the sight of the *kebeles*. When the mother threw herself on her son in order to protect him, they shoved her against the wall and snatched him from his bed. The last she saw of her son he was being dragged into the night by the collar of his pyjamas, crying out for his mother. The next day, his body was found four doors away. The woman never recovered from the shock; the last time I saw her she looked like a zombie.

Members of the Organization for African Unity and various embassies and foreign agencies witnessed firsthand the mass slaughter of children, yet there was no outcry. It is a sad and ugly chapter in the history of mankind.

My husband and I, along with the thousands of Eritreans then living in Addis, felt sickened and helpless living in a land drenched with the blood of its own children. For me, the city had become another prison, only this one was bigger and even harder to bear.

We began to seriously think about emigrating to the United States, where our children would be safe and where we would be able to work freely for the cause of Eritrean independence. There was no better way that Mesfun and I could serve my fellow prisoners, we reasoned, than by telling the outside world about what was going on. Since Eritrea still had a strong case at the United Nations, we were sure that it would not be difficult to bring the issue to the West.

Sister Weini, Saba, and a few of my other inmates had by this time been released. Fana and Berekti had been sentenced to five years. Genet was serving ten. Tsegga and Ribka had been transferred, at long last, to Haz Haz Prison. More and more women were making prison their home — the incarceration rate for women in Eritrea had taken an upward swing.

One afternoon in early August 1977, Mesfun picked me up at my office, as he usually did, at half past five. As he leaned over to open the car door for me, I noticed a bright smile, a rare sight since the Red Terror had begun.

"You seem happy. Good news from home?" I asked. Ethiopian National Radio never broadcast the truth about anything, much less about Eritrea, so we had to rely on word of mouth.

"Nothing new since last night," he replied. I searched his eyes for a sign of what it was that had made him beam so.

"The U.S. Department of Commerce is holding a seminar in Nairobi two months from now. It's for all commercial specialists in East Africa, so I've been invited."

"Does this mean you can leave the country legally?"

"Yes, but what is so great is that it will give us a chance to plan our escape!"

His trip to Nairobi, and our subsequent escape, would not be that easy, however. Several issues had to be addressed immediately.

In order to leave the country, even on a short business trip, every traveller had to find a guarantor who would put up fifty thousand dollars in case he or she failed to return. We agreed that I would be Mesfun's guarantor.

The only way that Muzit, Senait, and I could leave Ethiopia was to go to Asmara, slip into the liberated area, and then go on to Khartoum. But how was I going to get back home to Asmara?

The former governor of Eritrea, General Getachow Nadow, who had ordered my exile, had been murdered in June 1977 while he was in Addis Ababa for a meeting. It was widely rumored that the Dergue killed the General because he had suggested that mass killings had not been effective and that peaceful means should be considered in Eritrea.

Mesfun and I decided that I would first go to Asmara for a weekend, to test the waters since this turn of events. I would need a travel permit from our district kebele, however. We had been keeping a very low profile in Addis Ababa; we had not participated in kebele activities. Now I began attending meetings of the Women's Neighborhood Association, and it was not long before Mesfun and I were both considered members of the community in good standing. When the atmosphere seemed favorable, I had a friend talk to the chair of the local *kebele*, and then I applied. My permit was granted with the tacit proviso that I keep my movements in Asmara to a minimum.

On a Friday in mid-October 1977, I flew to Asmara. My father met me at the airport, and I spent a wonderful weekend with my family. Only close relatives and a few friends came to visit, and I left my parents' house only once, and then briefly. I flew back to Addis on Tuesday.

The chair of our *kebele* confided to my friend that the secret police had followed me in Asmara and that they had seen nothing unusual. This information served as assurance that I could return to Asmara without suspicion.

The third point that needed to be addressed before we left Ethiopia was the issue of the house that we loved so much in the Geza Banda area of Asmara. Under Ethiopian law, one was free to own a home but not to collect rent. Once Mesfun and the children moved out of our house and another family moved in, the government began collecting monthly rent. We agreed that we would leave the Asmara house as it was and forget the matter.

Mesfun's trip was scheduled for the twelfth of November. Coincidentally, on the eve of his departure the American Embassy threw a lavish party at the Hilton Hotel, and we were invited. While everyone else toasted the occasion — Marine Day —

Mesfun and I were dancing our farewell dance and celebrating the beginning of our escape from Ethiopia.

Mesfun flew to Nairobi, and after the seminar flew on to London, where he spent five days. Then he continued to Washington, D.C. As we had hoped, he received a warm welcome from our American friends. After reviewing the situation, he sent me the go-ahead, via a coded telegram, to proceed with our plan.

As it happened, Yoseph, my aunt's husband — who was also my contemporary and friend — came to Addis Ababa from Asmara on business. He was a committed underground member of the EPLF, and when I told him our secret he said he would be glad to help me get out of Asmara and to the liberated area. In the meantime, since Muzit and Senait were ready with their round-trip tickets to Asmara for the Christmas holidays, Yoseph volunteered to take them with him and he said that he would try to arrange for someone to meet me at the airport when I arrived. For the sake of their own safety, I did not tell my parents of my plans.

With my family all gone, and Christmas just a few days away, the time was right to approach the *kebele* for permission to spend the holidays in Asmara. The *kebele* officials were in the midst of a fund-raising campaign. Each woman was asked to make a straw basket, which would then be sold for five dollars. Anyone who could not produce one was required to pay out the five dollars herself. When I went to apply for the permit, they asked me when I planned to deliver my basket, and to their amazement I paid them twenty dollars instead of the required five. My permit was granted immediately, and two of the *kebele* members even asked me to convey their greetings to Mesfun.

Two days before leaving for Asmara, I invited a few of my women friends for an elaborate dinner and we all had a wonderful time. On the morning of my departure, I paid our maid her salary as well as a Christmas bonus.

I did not want to ask any of my close friends to drive me to the airport in case they were questioned when it was discovered that I had left for good. Instead, I casually asked an acquaintance who worked in another department at Ethiopian Airlines and who would never be taken for my accomplice.

When the plane finally took off at ten in the morning, after a two-hour delay, I surveyed Addis Ababa for the last time. It looked beautiful from the air, with its eucalyptus-covered hills, its wonderful buildings both ancient and modern, even its smoky little shacks. It was hard to believe that all this innocence and beauty was but a mask; that beneath it lay a place where unspeakable crimes were being committed daily, a place where the corpses of murdered children were left on the sidewalks.

Fifty-five minutes later I was home. There were more soldiers in evidence than there had been in October, and sandbags were visible on the roofs of all the airport buildings: a sign that the Dergue was nervous about our *tegadelti*. I was not eager to run into anyone I knew during this trip; I avoided people as much as possible and hid from friends and relatives, for I knew that when the authorities discovered that I had not returned after the permitted five days, they would start tracking me.

Yoseph had not succeeded in having me met at the airport. An acquaintance who had been on my flight offered me a lift to town, but I declined, and after waiting more than an hour I took a taxi to Yoseph's residence. There were very few people in the streets and to me they all looked frail. The taxi driver also looked a little haggard. I sat in front with him and we made small talk. When we passed the Expo Prison I blurted out, "There's the Expo." His demeanor changed and he murmured, "Yes, the Expo's still here." Every Eritrean knew about the heinous crimes committed at the Expo.

I did not want the taxi driver to drop me right in front of the house, so I got out some distance from the door and waited until he was out of sight. I rang the bell and when the maid opened the door, the first thing I noticed was the worn grass and dirt that had replaced their beautiful flowerbed and lawn.

Meaza, my aunt, was there to greet me, but my first cousins — who were only five and four years old — were at kindergarten. "Take off your shoes and lie down on the sofa until Yoseph comes home for lunch," suggested Meaza. "You must be tired from all that waiting at the airport." I noticed fine lines on Meaza's forehead and around her mouth that I had never seen before. She made herself comfortable on the couch in front of me. "Well, Yoseph has told me everything," she began. "Don't worry, we will work it out." Meaza always had her own special way of analyzing things.

"How was your trip?" she asked. "Did you have any trouble with the *kebeles*?"

"Not a bit," I replied.

"I'm so happy to see you," she went on, "but isn't it funny that after being away for so long, here you are at our place and not *Aiyei's!*" (*Aiyei* is a name given to a father-like figure — in this case Meaza's brother-in-law, my father.)

Indeed it was not only funny, but unnatural and ugly. I was an adult and my parents would never be held legally responsible for my actions under normal circumstances; these were not normal times. The memory of seeing *Abboi* thrown in jail just to put pressure on me was still fresh in my mind. Yoseph was a full-fledged member of the EPLF and their home was used by the *tegadelti* when they came from the field, so he and Meaza were more than willing to help their relatives. No one would have suspected them of helping me escape. My parents would be suspects immediately, and I wanted to avoid getting them into trouble if I could.

Meaza talked about how Asmara, the spirit of Europe in Africa, had been rendered lifeless by war and fear. She talked about a distant relative who had told her how the villagers were biding their time in silence, all the while working with their sons and daughters, the *tegadelti*.

Yoseph and the children finally came home; it was so good to see them. Sami and Minasie, my cousins, looked like twins even though they were a year apart. Meaza had prepared a dish with imported rice from the black market, and we all sat down to a wonderful meal. Yoseph talked mostly of the mess the Dergue had made in nationalizing companies, and of the new managers' crude ideas about communist ideological supremacy.

Yoseph returned to work. I talked with the children for a while, and then we all retired for an afternoon nap. Later, the maid prepared tea and *hambasha* and Meaza and I settled down for a chat.

Meaza confided that she was very worried about Yoseph. Between his demanding job and his EPLF activities, it was only at mealtimes that he had the chance to sit down. When he was at home, she said, he was always either on the telephone or listening to the radio, turning the dial compulsively from one station to the next. He was so on edge that he was running the house for her, worrying about every little housekeeping detail. Even with all these pressures, though, I had noticed that Yoseph was still patient with his children.

We talked of family — brothers, sisters, aunts, and uncles — but mostly we talked about my mother.

"She's always afraid that the *afagn* will take Dawit and Michael, and she gets absolutely frantic if they're not home at least a half hour before curfew," said Meaza. "She paces up and down in the compound. And the longing for her children abroad is so sad."

"Mother has not been the same since I was imprisoned." I agreed, "and now her grandchildren suddenly disappearing won't help at all. But what choice do we have?"

When she began telling me about the many youths who were joining the fronts, my thoughts naturally turned to my Ruth and Tamar.

"Meaza " I began. "You know how our children have been brought up; how sheltered they've been. Do you think Ruth and Tamar know much, you know, about the movement... other than what is just common knowledge?" I posed this question very haltingly.

"You have two bright girls," replied Meaza. "Regardless of how protective you have tried to be, they've lived in Asmara all their lives, and they've been going to public high school for almost a year. I'd be surprised, frankly, if they're not involved in the underground movement."

I brushed the idea aside and changed the subject. I did not want to believe what Meaza was telling me.

In the evening when Yoseph came home, the three of us began plotting how we would bring my children from their grandparents' house and how we would get through the checkpoint at the edge of town. It was decided that Yoseph would pick up the girls in the morning under the pretext of having them over for the day. As for the checkpoint, we agreed that we should dress like peasants and say we were just returning home to our village: At that time, villagers were not required to carry identification cards. We knew, however, that even if we dressed the part, there was the chance that our faces would give us away.

"Don't worry," said Yoseph. "The guards at the checkpoint are not incorruptible. I'll find somebody to arrange safe conduct."

Just before dinner, at around eight o'clock, we heard the sound of gunfire. "The soldiers in Kagnew Station and the Selassamestegna [the thirty-fifth brigade] are firing out of fear that the *tegadelti* might attack them," Yoseph said.

The next morning at ten o'clock, Yoseph went to my parents' home to get the children. I became restless in the house, so I went out to the compound to wait for them. Meaza followed me outside and chatted to distract me. We both knew that telling my children of the escape plan was going to be no easy matter.

Then who should come by but Tekie, my uncle. When he noticed how I was dressed and that my hair had been braided so that I would look like a typical rural housewife, he got the message immediately, and the three of us went inside to discuss my plans. Tekie volunteered to accompany us until we reached the liberated city of Keren. He was a merchant and his truck had been confiscated by the Dergue because he had been accused of aiding the *tegadelti* by transporting grain. His truck taken away, he existed only on small trade.

At about a quarter to eleven I heard a car door slam and then the sound of footsteps. My heart started pounding and my eyes met Meaza's. My children ran toward me. They were all surprised, of course, and puzzled as to why I was at Meaza and Yoseph's house and not at their grandparents'.

Tekie greeted my daughters, and then he and Yoseph went to discuss the plan together, taking great care to leave no loose ends. After that, Yoseph left to survey the checkpoint, and my uncle went home to change clothes for the journey. Tekie had managed to get in and out of Asmara and travel to Keren many times.

In that sunny living room, I sat with Ruth and Tamar at my sides, while Muzit and Senait sat on the floor leaning their heads on my knees. I did not give them a chance to bombard me with questions, but plunged on ahead. First I gave them news of their friends in Addis; then I told them about how easy it had been for me to get my travel permit from the *kebeles,* and so on — I thought I would ease into it. But they were still looking baffled. I cleared my throat, fought hard to remain cool, and launched into the subject as though I were in a formal meeting:

"My dear children, your father continued on to America from Nairobi. I have had to keep this to myself until now for the sake of our safety. As you know, things have been getting very dangerous for us and the many Eritreans living in Ethiopia. On top of everything else, it is rumored that a concentration camp is being built for the Eritreans and the Tigreans. So before your father's departure, we decided to escape and emigrate to the United States until total liberation has been achieved. You will be able to continue your education safely and without interruption; and we will be able to help the struggle freely and more effectively. But we must begin our escape this morning — right away."

The room grew perfectly silent.

"What about our friends? Can't we go back and say good-bye to them?" Muzit asked, with a frown much too serious for her years. "Mommy, what are you talking about?" asked Ruth. "Tamar and I are in the EPLF and we have important assignments to carry out. We can't pick up and leave Asmara just like that." I looked straight into her eyes and saw determination. I glanced at Tamar and read the same message.

Ruth's statement stirred mixed feelings in me. On the one hand I was happily surprised to hear that they were involved, because given their Western-style and sheltered upbringing we had doubted that they understood what the struggle was all about. On the other hand, I certainly did not want to leave them behind. So I collected myself and said:

"It is very honorable of you to fight for your motherland in any way that you can. There is just one problem. Once the authorities know I'm gone, you will be the first ones to be detained, and heaven knows you could never withstand the inter-rogation." As I said this, my own prison experience flashed through my mind, I thought of all that I had gone through and witnessed, and what Ribka — who was only three years older than Ruth — had told me about teenagers being killed and buried in the grounds of the Expo Prison.

I gave my children only two hours to get ready. They could not say goodbye to their friends. It seemed cruel, but that was the only way; if the news leaked out it would be disastrous. Never mind, I consoled myself, they will understand when the time comes.

Yoseph and Tekie went over the plan again and came to the conclusion that it would be best to tell the guards we were going to a wedding in a nearby village. We all put on our disguises and ended up looking plausibly like a family going off to a rural wedding; Meaza even wrapped up some perfume as the gift in case we were required to provide proof. The four girls, in their simple outfits and with their sad, confused faces, looked like refugees already.

We all gathered in the compound, except Meaza, who stayed behind for fear of revealing her emotions. Tekie left first, carrying our meager ration of clothing in a plastic bag; he would be taking a bus to a point not far from the checkpoint.

"Quick," said Yoseph, hurrying us to the car. "We're taking too much time." His sons were trying to stall the inevitable departure, hugging the girls and talking idly until the bitter end.

Finally, we all got in the car. I sat in front with Senait on my lap; Muzit, Tamar, and Ruth settled in the back seat. Meaza whisked the two boys inside and Yoseph started the engine.

Only the main street of Godiaf, Yoseph and Meaza's neighborhood, was paved, so we drove along the gravel road and in a few seconds reached the main highway. The sky was clear and the sun was brilliant. Asmara seemed even quieter than it had been when I arrived two days before, the only sound being the persistent whir of a helicopter for several minutes. As we neared the checkpoint, however, there seemed to be much more life; perhaps it was the neighborhood children, who were shouting and playing ball.

I felt little hands on my shoulders.

"Mommy, can't we even say goodbye to Grandma and Grandpa?" Muzit pleaded.

As I turned around to soothe her, my Muzit looked like one of the orphans I once taught who always seemed to expect a vague answer to her questions, or no answer at all. The anger I saw in Ruth's eyes at that moment, and in Tamar's as well, was no less disturbing.

"Cheer up, my young friends," offered Yoseph. "Try to understand why your mother has to do this. Eritrea will be free soon, then we will all be together again."

He turned to me: "Be sure to give my regards to

Mesfun...and don't get too Americanized," he joked. Looking ahead and behind, right and left, we got out quickly.

"*Ciao.* Good luck," Yoseph added, and he sped off, taking a different route to go home.

We walked toward several people sitting on the sidewalk some twenty yards from the checkpoint where the guards were posted. There were about forty people in all, most of them women villagers. Of the few men, two had the appearance of city-dwellers. There was no one I knew personally.

The checkpoint rules were constantly changing at the whim of the guards or their supervisors, and that particular morning one of the guards had decided that nobody at all was going to go through. Some of the people had been waiting since early morning. After about an hour, Tekie joined us. He had given the plastic bag containing our clothes to a man who regularly went by horse and cart to the area around Embaderho to get vegetables to sell in Asmara. For an agreed price Tekie had arranged to hide our clothes under the seat of his cart.

People were getting restless, especially those who had been waiting since early morning. My children were bored and fidgety. At three o'clock in the afternoon, four city women gave up. "Fools. Idiots. Murderers. They're wasting my time," I heard one of them say through clenched teeth as she passed me on her way back from the checkpoint. Even the man with the horse and cart was not getting through that day. Tekie, who was constantly on the lookout, said it would be better if we walked about instead of staying in one spot. The exit was in a vast field, but it would have been dangerous to try going around the checkpoint, not only because of the armed guards but also because we feared there were land mines.

At about four o'clock, the guard who had arbitrarily decided to close the exit left for the day, and then things changed. The remaining two guards started admitting those people who appeared to be trying to get home to their villages.

It was getting late, and my daughters were getting more and more restless as they nibbled at the sandwiches and *hambasha* that we had packed. Finally Tekie negotiated with the guards through his contact. We were told indirectly to pretend we were from the area and were just going to draw water from a well some hundred yards away. The guards generally would not bother anyone past the checkpoint for fear of the *tegadelti* who were known to be in the area.

Two women who were actually going for water let Ruth and Tamar carry their buckets, and the girls made it through with no questions asked. Then it was my turn, and I made it too!

Muzit and Senait were left with Tekie. Ruth, Tamar, and I patiently waited for them at the well. We noticed that neighborhood children would sneak in and out of the checkpoint bringing buckets back and forth so that people in the line could pose as local residents. It occurred to me as I watched them that the action of these children represented its own unique form of resistance.

Finally, at half past six, the guards became so tired of being asked by one person after another that they decided to let everybody cross. By that time there were close to sixty people. As the crowd streamed through, I spotted Tekie and my Muzit and Senait coming towards us!

The tension of the day seemed to melt away. We all hugged and let out a collective sigh of relief. Tekie's face literally shone, the girls looked less resentful, and Muzit apparently resolved to ask no more questions.

Tekie's contact, with the horse and cart, crossed the checkpoint, and we paid him to give us a ride from Adi Abeito to Embaderho. From Embaderho we would walk to Serajaka and then take an EPLF bus at night to Keren, a totally liberated city.

In Mai Hutsa, as we all sat squeezed together in the cart, I saw for the first time four fully-armed *tegadelti*. Total liberation seemed so near at hand that it was almost tangible.

The excitement was barely over when we reached Embaderho.

As we began the walk, I was suddenly hit by a bombshell from Ruth: she said she wanted to go to Medrizen to meet the recruitment leader and join the *tegadelti*. I did not give her a chance to say another word. I was furious. We stared into each other's eyes for quite some time, until finally Ruth relented and cast her eyes downward.

I eventually cooled off and we continued the walk in silence, the four of us helping Muzit and Senait when they lagged behind.

Soon after we arrived in Serajaka, it grew pitch black. The only light came from a quarter moon and the stars, augmented by fires here and there in the bus stop area: neighborhood girls were making tea and selling it to passengers for twenty-five cents a cup. The bus was supposed to arrive at half past ten, but eleven o'clock came and went and there was no sign of it. The air got chilly so we clustered around a small fire.

Ruth, who was angry because of my reaction to her idea, did not so much as open her mouth. Tamar was unusually quiet. I could tell that Muzit already missed her home and her grandparents. Even Senait was more subdued than normal. They were all totally exhausted.

We are out of reach of the enemy, in a liberated zone, I thought to myself. We were so happy when we crossed the checkpoint. What is bothering me? I wondered. Is it simply fear of the unknown? It was so good to breathe free air, yet I was seized by panic. Had I done the right thing, whisking the children away from the only life they had ever known?

I sat there in the dark, waiting for a bus to take us to I knew not what kind of life, my two young ones too exhausted to be comforted, and my two older ones in no mood to communicate whatever it was they were feeling. The emotional turmoil was too much; my eyes were getting misty and I could feel a lump forming in my throat. I had to get away from myself and those nagging doubts and fears. I stood up, took a *netsela* out of our plastic bag, and placed it over the children's backs to keep them warm. But there was nowhere to walk. There were some thirty passengers crowded into the small waiting area confined on one side by the fields and on the other by the highway just a few yards away.

Two of the three armed *tegadelti* guarding the passengers warmed themselves over a small fire and chatted with Tekie. The other stood alone. A cloth covered his mouth and he had on an old jacket that looked too worn to protect him from the night air. He noticed that I wanted to talk.

"I gather that you are the mother of the four girls," he began, "but you don't look old enough for that." He let the cloth fall down around his neck so he would be heard.

"So I guess you are going to America," he observed after

some rudimentary conversation. He did not wait for me to elaborate, though. Instead he launched into the one subject that was on the agenda in Eritrea at all times: our independence.

"Let's face it. The story of Eritrea is a special one, and a very sad one," he said. "Why did the U.S.-dominated United Nations support the idea of an Eritrea federated with Ethiopia, back in the 1950s, when other African countries like Somalia and Libya were granted independence?" Our going to America seemed to have sparked off this tirade against the United States and the West.

"By being colonized for so long, by the Italians for fifty years and then the British for ten, we developed a large working class, and we even had our own parliament and our own flag. Can't we be left alone to lead our nation?

"Tell me this: How could we be expected to live peacefully with feudal Ethiopia? And why did the U.N. and the U.S. close their eyes when, despite the U.N. decision, Eritrea was annexed in the 1960s and declared the fourteenth Ethiopian province? I just cannot figure it out. It is so maddening.

"After all peaceful negotiations had failed, after our parliament had been dismantled, after our language had been outlawed and Amharic, that... that imperial language, forced on us — what is wrong with taking up arms to fight for self-determination? That is our right. " He pursed his lips and shook his head in a gesture of bafflement.

"Why are the United Nations and the United States — the whole world, for that matter — ignoring us even now, when victory is obviously just around the corner? Oh, they say, it's just one group of black African Marxists against another. How can they be so cynical?"

The *tegadalai* was merely voicing the frustration that we all felt to various degrees and would discuss for hours on end; but this soulful plea from that frustrated young patriot held special significance for me on that chilly night, in that little patch of gravel among the few dozen or so bedraggled travellers in liberated Eritrea. I was feeling like a dispossessed, displaced person myself. I desperately needed to make sense of my world. "Ethiopia says it needs access to the sea, the ports of Assab and Massawa , but is there not a peaceful means, a negotiation of some sort?" I offered, trying to put it into some sort of perspective.

"Ethiopia was always a strong ally of the West, particularly the United States. The West cannot figure out what kind of government Eritrea will end up having if we are allowed to become totally independent. They felt safe with their imperial ally.

"But you are absolutely right," I went on. "The fate of three and a half million people cannot be decided by others — it is so wrong, so unjust — and all that human suffering."

The *tegadalai* seemed to have had enough of the subject for the moment. "Combat takes up all your attention, physical and mental. But an assignment like this, as a guard, can be really boring. All kinds of thoughts come into your head."

I noticed that he had been glancing over at Ruth and Tamar frequently.

"How old are you?" I asked.

"Twenty-four."

"And when did you join the *tegadelti*?"

"In 1975 — from Europe, where I was working towards my degree in agriculture. My girlfriend was Danish. She looked something like one of your daughters."

Tamar is light-skinned, so I figured it must have been her who resembled his girlfriend. I looked at my daughters. Muzit and Senait were curled up in the arms of their sisters. Through the flickering light of the fire they looked beautiful, even in their utter exhaustion. Tamar looked pink in the yellow glow of the flame.

"Her mother liked me," continued the young *tegadalai*.

"There would have been no problem there if we had gotten married, but I wonder how my parents would have reacted," he said longingly.

"Do you still keep in touch with her?"

"No. When I left she said, 'You are going to be so involved in the struggle, you'll be married to your country.' 'Maybe I just won't live long enough to get married,' I told her."

Towards the end of our conversation he was having trouble keeping his eyes off Tamar. I could imagine him stroking the hair of his Danish girlfriend and kissing her, back there on the campus of some European university.

The other two *tegadelti*, rifles mounted on their shoulders, constantly on the watch, kept to themselves except when my uncle would wander over to pass the time with them. I learned later from Tekie that one was a farmer, and he had learned to read since joining the struggle. The other had been a high school student when he joined the EPLF. Tekie kept himself busy the entire evening. If he was not talking with the two *tegadelti* he was teasing Ruth and Tamar, and he entertained Muzit and Senait with jokes until they were quite sleepy. He would jump up whenever he thought he heard the humming of the bus, and he hurried us to get ready for boarding when it finally did arrive.

Tekie carried Senait, I helped my still drowsy Muzit. Tamar and Ruth straightened their clothes and pulled their *netselas* over their foreheads, and we all boarded. There were far more passengers than the bus could accommodate, and the five of us had to squeeze into three seats. Tekie had to stand, clinging to the iron rod that ran along the ceiling. Muzit and Senait dozed off almost immediately.

The packed bus started rolling at a quarter past midnight. It was pitch black and I marveled at the skill of the *tegadalai* driver as he negotiated the many twists and turns of the mountain road, often with the headlights turned off in order to evade detection by the Ethiopian army. We stopped in many villages, passengers getting off and disappearing into the night, and others boarding. At the bus stops, young boys and girls sold nuts, boiled eggs, and homemade bread to the passengers.

I tried to start a conversation with Ruth and Tamar. Although for a brief moment after we had crossed the checkpoint I had seen relief on their faces, I sensed that they were still not willing to talk. The tension between us was beginning to affect me. I had looked forward so much to sharing these special first moments of freedom with my little brood.

To the sound of the engine and the chatter of the passengers, I withdrew into myself and reflected on my family. It had been my father's dream to retire in a few years, to have his sons take over and expand his tanning factory. My thoughts ran to my mother, who had reached the age when she should have been pampered by her children; but instead of the many grandchildren she wanted, even the four she did have, were now being snatched away.

My mind wandered back to the discussion with the

*tegadalai,* and I thought about the myth of Ethiopian territorial integrity. Since when had Eritrea been part of Ethiopia? At one time or another, Eritrea had been ruled by Turks, Arabs, Egyptians, Italians, and the British. Would all of these countries now lay claim to us? Was not all of Africa colonized by one power or another, and were not all of its borders created by the colonials? Where is the legitimacy of Ethiopia's ruling Eritrea? Were we Eritreans born to be forever dominated? At the end of the Second World War, when the British defeated Italy in Eritrea, we received them as liberators with open arms. But they betrayed our dreams. In a temporary ten-year trusteeship over Eritrea, the British undermined our economy and our infrastructure; then they closed their eyes when Ethiopia and other countries claimed that we were not economically viable, supported Ethiopia's need to have access to the sea, and conveniently trusted the Emperor's pronouncement that he was "protecting" Eritrea's interests.

I could not help but ask myself: why were three and a half million Eritreans considered dispensable by the United Nations and the West? Was it fate, or was it truly a lack of justice on the part of the United Nations?

One scene after another invaded my mind: the five hundred wounded and eighty killed during a demonstration by the Eritrean labor movement in 1958; the one hundred and ten villages destroyed in the lowlands in 1967, with the ensuing mass exodus to Sudan; the five hundred killed in Woki just a few miles from Asmara in early 1975. And then the Palace Prison. The spine-chilling cry of the child who had been imprisoned with his mother, the disfigured faces and swollen feet of the interrogated inmates, my cellmates at the Palace and at Haz Haz.

I worried about the fate of my brothers Dawit and Michael: The *afagn* are always on the lookout for strong young men. And if Ruth and Tamar were involved in the underground, Lia must be too. It was very possible that my brothers were involved. Oh God, protect them! I saw Mesfun at that very moment fretting over our exit, and pacing the floor wherever he was in the United States.

With still nothing said between my daughters and myself, we arrived in Keren at two a.m. and flopped down for the night in a crowded hotel. We all slept until late the next morning. The children looked much better after a good night's sleep and a shower — even if their dresses were still a mass of wrinkles. Ruth's face no longer betrayed the anger of the previous evening; but I drew a deep breath when I looked at her for the first time that day, for only then did I remember that a wedge had been driven between us. It clearly was not going to be easy to deal with the differences that were developing between me and my two rapidly maturing teenagers.

At ten o'clock we moved to a more comfortable hotel, had breakfast in a restaurant, and walked a little.

Tekie then left immediately to make the long and harrowing return trip to Asmara, promising to return to Keren before it was time for us to move on.

# Fourteen

The beautiful liberated city of Keren, the pride of every Eritrean, was our undeclared capital at the time of our long and tortuous journey from Asmara to the West.

Towering over Keren are the Lalemba Hills and a giant fort built during the days of the Italian colonization. The main streets are lined with Italian-style houses, their gardens overflowing with flowering shrubs; then there are the smaller, two- or three-roomed white-washed houses, some of them scattered over the hills as well; and, lower down on the social scale — the modest thatched-roof homes of the poor farmers. A beautiful ornamental garden takes a place of honor in the center of town. The Catholic churches, most of them built during the Italian period, and the mosques, their domes catching the brilliant northeast African sun, gives the town its distinctive flavor.

The city suffered considerable damage during the battle for liberation — schools, hospitals, churches, and mosques were bombed. The EPLF, with its skilled labor, would have been able to repair the buildings and restore Keren, but the constant threat of the Dergue's air power and the lack of funds made it impossible for the present.

By the time my daughters and I had returned from our walk the morning after our arrival in Keren, Ruth seemed relaxed, much to my relief. Telling the girls I would not be long, I went to the EPLF public administration office, not only to discuss my travel plans but to pay a social call as well.

A thin, stooped man greeted me in a friendly way at the EPLF office. He asked about my family and said he was glad to see that we were still alive considering the indiscriminate persecutions that the Dergue had been carrying out in Asmara. I was taken by surprise, for I had no idea who this person was. When he told me who he was, I could hardly believe it! The tough life of a *tegadalai* really does take its toll, I thought — for before me stood Mesfun's friend Tesfai, the elegant socialite who had once frequented the cocktail parties and dinners at the Officers' Club in Kagnew Station. He was now skin and bones. The rifle that he carried on his shoulder seemed far too heavy for his frail body.

As he started sharing his experiences, however, I forgot about Tesfai's outward appearance and saw a giant of a person. He told me about the life of the *tegadelti*, about their acts of bravery against all odds — outnumbered, outgunned, starving, ill-clad, unprotected against the scorching sun and the desert cold. Tesfai had not heard from his wife and three children for some time, but he seemed resigned to a life away from them. At least his children had a mother who earned a salary and would take care of them, Tesfai said — that is, unless she had been thrown in prison. We talked about the concentration camp for Eritreans and Tigreans rumored to be under construction in Addis Ababa, and we chatted at length about my imprisonment in Asmara. Then I told Tesfai my plans. He suggested I stay in Keren and let Mesfun do what he could from America, (for the EPLF always discourages Eritreans from becoming refugees abroad.) I explained that we were sure we could better serve the struggle in exile. The aging fighter said that he would discuss our case with the person responsible for such matters, and that in the meantime he would be coming to the hotel to see the children.

I went back to the hotel bursting with news about our old friend and full of excitement at the prospect of sitting down with the children to plan the rest of our trip, out of Eritrea, to Sudan, and Europe, then on to America. My elation was short-lived, however, for I learned that Ruth and Tamar had news of their own.

They had gone to the EPLF recruitment office and joined up.

I was speechless. I pulled myself together and tried to tell the girls that, given their background and upbringing, they were bound to be more of a burden than a help to the struggle. When this fell on deaf ears, I lectured them on the importance of higher education, not only for themselves but to a future independent Eritrea.

"I know that, Mother," began Ruth, sounding very much

the adult all of a sudden. "But first we have to have a country where we can live peacefully. Only then should we think about our education." Tamar nodded her agreement.

Muzit and Senait had no idea of the gravity of the matter under discussion, and they kept interrupting us in a bid for my attention.

I had to leave them all and go off to think by myself. I paced the sidewalk in front of the hotel, under the perfumed bougainvillaea. I understood Ruth and Tamar, of course, I told myself. After all, Mesfun and I had risked our lives for the cause; in fact, we considered it our duty to do so. I would have gladly joined the front myself, if I were younger, I admitted. Perhaps I should be supporting their decision. I was torn. But in the end the maternal instinct proved to be stronger than mere reason. I wanted my daughters to be safe.

At five o'clock a *tegadalai* came to see me from the recruitment office while Muzit and Senait were playing in the hotel compound. We talked briefly about our trip from Asmara to Keren, and then he came to the purpose of his visit.

"Your children have decided to join the Eritrean People's Liberation Army," he said casually.

"Yes, but give them a week in the blistering heat and they'll change their minds. I know they will never make it."

We were both quiet for several seconds; neither Ruth nor Tamar dared contribute anything to the minor battle taking place. The *tegadelai* broke the silence: "There are hundreds like them who have never even seen the countryside before. But you have no idea how quickly they adapt to the new life. Your children will survive it. The love of a motherland is strong enough for them to endure whatever hardships they have to face."

But I was in no mood to talk. The *tegadalai* soon stood to leave, telling the girls he would be seeing them before their departure, and I accompanied him to the entrance of the hotel.

"You are an Eritrean mother," he said, "and you share the lot of thousands of other mothers. Besides, they are of age now. You have no choice but to respect their decision."

Tears welled up in my eyes. The seasoned fighter was at a loss for words. Perhaps he was thinking of his own mother, for his eyes turned red and he slowed his gait. "Unless the enemy is totally defeated and peace prevails, death and suffering and family separation will be the lot of every Eritrean," he said.

"How well I know," I replied. "Who would have thought just a few days ago that Ruth and Tamar would become *tegadelti*?"

That evening we made dinner in our room and I tried to be cheerful, but we ate with little interest and went to bed early. In the morning, while the children still slept, I went to Mass at St. Mary's Church and then sat alone at the back of the church for a while. I returned to find that Ruth and Tamar had cut off their long hair and were preparing to leave. They had bathed their sisters and tidied the room.

It was too much for me to bear. I turned immediately and went back to church, this time to St. Michael's. But Mass was over and the church was closed. Even the tranquillity of the churchyard — the singing of the birds, the gentle breeze, the infinite blue sky, the Lalemba Hills in the distance — could not calm my anguish. In my mind I saw my girls carrying guns and dropping from exhaustion in the desert. How I wished my mother or my father or Mesfun were with me. I felt so alone and desolate.

I cannot recall exactly what I said to Ruth and Tamar when I got back to the hotel, but I remember that we avoided each other's eyes and that both Muzit and Senait looked sad. Later, I bought Ruth and Tamar each two bedsheets, plastic sandals, and sanitary napkins: that was all they needed. Tamar removed her silver ring and slipped it onto Muzit's middle finger. They took off their gold earrings and the watches that Tekie had hidden when we crossed the checkpoint and later gave them to me. I put the watches on my wrists; I clung to these mementoes for a very long time to come.

I had wanted the five of us to have our last meal together, in our room; but since I was not able to hold back the tears I let them eat alone and went back to church for a while.

At four o'clock, they were to leave for the transportation depot. They already looked like *tegadelti* with their hair cut short and wearing plastic sandals, an EPLF trademark.

We closed the door to our room and walked in silence to the depot as though marching in a funeral procession. I kept telling myself that what they were doing was right and noble, that I was proud of them; but several steps before we reached the depot I stopped suddenly and began to turn back, taking Muzit and Senait by the hand. With eyes cast downward I mumbled my goodbyes. Tamar grabbed me by the shoulders and insisted that we embrace and say farewell properly. I could not control my emotions any longer. We all clung to each other and wept, cheek to cheek, hands clutching. Muzit and Senait were brokenhearted. Even though their sisters had spoken to them at length about their mission when I had been out, they still did not fully comprehend. They both cried so inconsolably that they attracted the attention of passersby, and several children gathered around to see what was going on.

Apparently this was not the first time such a scene had taken place outside the transportation depot, for a woman came up to us. "These must be your daughters," she said. "Please don't cry. Take heart. One day soon they will proudly march into Asmara under the banner of freedom."

Eventually we had to release each other and Ruth and Tamar continued on to the EPLF depot, while we three walked home slowly, feeling sad and dejected.

At half past seven that evening there was a knock at the door. Who could it possibly be? I wondered. I opened the door and for a second I thought I was dreaming, for there stood Ruth and Tamar!

"Did you change your minds, or did the recruitment office change its mind about you?" I asked, my heart racing.

"The truck was full. We are scheduled to go tomorrow," Ruth answered with a weak smile.

Muzit and Senait jumped from Tamar to Ruth and from Ruth to Tamar. It was wonderful to have them back, even if it was for just one night. I decided to make the best of that bonus time together and to give my brave daughters a joyous farewell. But it was now Ruth and Tamar's turn to comfort their mother, and I was touched by how sweet they were, how understanding of my sorrow. How I wished they could stay just one more week.

The next morning we were joined by an acquaintance who lightened the mood with jokes about EPLF recruits. We had lunch at a restaurant, and in sharp contrast to the dismal mood of the previous day, we were less tense when we walked once more to the transportation depot.

Although I was hardly delighted with how my plans were turning out, my emotions were now under control. When everyone was told to get into the truck, we again fell into each other's arms. Holding my daughters, one at a time, tightly to my chest until I could feel their heartbeat, is among the experiences that I shall never forget. Muzit and Senait stalled the farewell as long as they could, clinging passionately to their sisters. Then Ruth and Tamar climbed aboard and the truck pulled away. We waved until they were out of sight.

We dawdled all the way back to the hotel, stopping at a coffee shop to buy cookies but saying very little. When we got to our room, the three of us sat silently on the bed, Muzit slipping the ring that Tamar had given her on and off her finger. That evening we pushed the beds together and slept with Muzit on my left and Senait on my right. They needed my consolation, and I needed theirs. I was lonesome.

We lay awake a long time. At last Muzit asked:

"Do you think they are in Sahel yet, Mommy?"

"Well, Sahel is a vast area," I replied. "I don't know the exact location of the training center. If not today, they will be there tomorrow."

"Maybe they'll come back again, just like last night!" suggested the ever hopeful Senait, perhaps speaking for the three of us.

In the morning we had a surprise visitor.

"In the name of heavens, is that you, Alemseged?" I exclaimed with arms outstretched. Alemseged was a good friend of my brothers Petros and Paulos, and he had worked on the research committee of our Relief and Rehabilitation Association for Eritrea.

"I just heard last night that you were here. I couldn't wait to see you," he said.

A young man of just over thirty at that time, Alemseged was full of life and humor. He had been educated in the United States but was very much a revolutionary. He was like a brother to me.

"I heard that you participated in the Adi Nefas battle just three months after you joined the front," I said.

"Forget the battles," replied Alemseged with characteristic modesty, resting his rifle against the wall and kissing Muzit and Senait. He marveled at how they had grown since he had seen them last, almost three years ago.

"When did you come to Keren, Abeba? Where are Mesfun and your other two?"

"Mesfun is in America." I hesitated a moment. "...And Ruth and Tamar went to Sahel for training yesterday. Do you think they'll get through it?"

"Yes, of course they will! You have no idea how quickly the city youngsters adapt, Abeba. It is really something."

"But Alemseged, you know how Tamar and Ruth were brought up!"

"Don't worry. Honest. I swear to you they will adapt. No doubt."

"Do you think that, you know, being girls... that they will have to participate in actual combat?"

"Oh, maybe not," he replied.

I knew very well that girls took part in combat, even on the front lines, but I preferred to fool myself.

Alemseged was posted to the education department of the EPLF and he told me about the programs that were being conducted, including an extensive literacy campaign. "But our resources are so limited. There is a shortage of everything, from pens and pencils to textbooks — you name it," he sighed.

We had so many things to talk about. I reminded him about the morning in November 1974 when he came to my office grim-faced and slumped into a chair without saying a word. He had just heard about the fifty students who were strangled to death with piano wire by the *afagn*. Only weeks later Alemseged would join the struggle.

I had heard a few months previously when we were living in Addis Ababa that his father had passed away in Asmara; and I did not want to bring up the subject of Alemseged's family now, for fear that he had not heard the news.

"I see that you are carefully avoiding the subject of my family," he said. "I've heard that father died recently, Abeba. Is that what you are trying to hide?"

I could see the pain in his eyes, yet Alemseged tried to be

cheerful, as always. Perhaps remembering the words of Martin Luther King from his days as a graduate student in the United States, he said: "We shall overcome" as he stood and picked up his gun to leave.

We stayed two weeks in Keren after that, which gave me time to meet many people, mostly women, streaming in from every corner of Eritrea — and even from Addis Ababa — in search of information about their husbands, their daughters, their sons: the *tegadelti*.

Muzit and Senait grew bored after their sisters left us; my lengthy conversations with EPLF members and the families of fighters meant very little to them. They had a wonderful time, though, when we went to visit my friends at the convent school, where they feasted on such rare treats as home-baked cakes and candy. They were especially thrilled when an old school chum of mine honored us with the traditional meal of chicken *tsebhi* with eggs that is served only on very special occasions. Muzit didn't care for chicken *tsebhi*, but she was thrilled to find a girl her own age to play with. Then they had to wait for my Uncle Tekie's arrival from Asmara four days before our departure to be teased and entertained and made much of once again.

Everywhere I went, with whomever I spoke, the discussion centred around one subject — the possibility of Russian involvement in the war. The air was filled with such questions as: "The Soviet Union advocated Eritrean independence in the 1940s; is it not going to be difficult for it to change its position now?" and "Why did the Russians abandon Somalia, their long-time ally, and make an about-face to side with Ethiopia as soon as the Americans left?"

"Being a refugee will not be easy," said the EPLF official who came to see us off for Sudan. "Think of the *manjus* [an EPLF term for "young fighters"], and do whatever you can to help the struggle from America."

My uncle kept waving until we were out of sight. He could not help but become emotional at the very end, and so did I.

The journey to Sudan took three days. We rested the first night in Afabet, a small town north of Keren. The second day we stayed in a place that looked like no-man's-land and drove in the late afternoon and at night in order to avoid not only the scorching sun, but also the air raids that were a constant danger including border areas. Passengers and *tegadelti* boarded and disembarked at many points, but only my two children and I, a man of about thirty, and three girls — one of them with her eight-year-old nephew — were going on to Sudan. We all felt secure as long as we were in the EPLF truck and on our own soil. But as soon as we left the Eritrean side of Karora and crossed to Karora, Sudan, and were handed over to the Sudanese officials by an EPLF representative, we felt like orphans.

It was early afternoon when we arrived, and the Sudanese officials put us up in a one-room house, which was the filthiest place I had ever seen — with the exception, of course, of the toilet at the Palace Prison. I tried to sweep sand over the feces that were scattered liberally throughout the nasty little yard, while the girls swept the room.

The room was bare but for four beds and a few pots and pans, but at least we could prepare tea. I had brought bread from Keren, and I had some dates, oranges, and powdered milk for Muzit and Senait and the young boy. There were eight of us and only four beds, and we had to give one of them to the only man among us, who had begun flirting shamelessly with one of the three girls.

Suddenly, in the middle of the night, I was awakened from my sleep by loud banging on the door. My God! I thought. We are out of reach of the *afagn*. What on earth could be going on? During the daylight hours I had noticed that the dirty walls of our room were covered in graffiti, written in Tigrinya: "It is hell to be a refugee" — "I love you, Mother. Please forgive me for leaving you" — "Oh, Mother Eritrea, what have we done to you?" — and, most significant for me at this frightening moment: "Beware of the Sudanese officials; they are always looking for women."

Our male roommate was fast asleep. The knocking persisted. None of the children budged from their sleep, but all three of the girls woke in terror.

I went to the door and without opening it asked who was there. A male voice replied, in broken English, that he had been appointed our guardian and had come to count us. Oh, fine, I thought: the British and the Ethiopians had appointed themselves the guardians of Eritrea, and here we now have a Sudanese guardian!

"Why do you have to count us in the middle of the night?" I asked. "We are eight. Then I turned to our male companion and said, "Wake up, friend!"

"He is not looking for me," he answered, to my astonishment and utter disgust, he went back to sleep.

The intruder finally left when I threatened to report him.

The next day we boarded a truck and were accompanied by a Sudanese official and a policeman to the town of Toker, a drive of some five or six hours from Karora, where we would be quarantined for six days. Our quarters this time were absolute hell for Muzit and Senait. There was not even a bed. I had brought two blankets with me and we used these for the three children; the rest of us slept on a concrete floor covered by a straw mat.

Because we were under quarantine, our movements were restricted, and we were not allowed to leave the premises even to purchase food. The medical officer assigned to check us while we waited for our papers was kind enough, fortunately, to procure some decent food for the children; otherwise I don't know what we would have done. He offered to take Muzit and Senait home with him, for he had daughters their age; but the police would not allow them to leave until the quarantine period was up and the papers complete.

At long last, after six days, we boarded an EPLF truck that would take us from Toker to Port Sudan. Priority was always given to children and the sick on EPLF trucks, so my girls and I got to sit in the cab with the driver. It struck me as he told how he had almost lost his life in battle, that the *tegadelti* were never happy about surviving; rather, they invariably wished that they had been killed and their comrades spared! It is quite remarkable.

Once we arrived in Port Sudan and were placed in EPLF lodgings, I sent a telegram to Mesfun. He called immediately from Washington and I felt my stomach tighten the instant I heard his voice.

"Are you alright?" he asked.

"You don't sound yourself at all. Has the trip worn you out?"

"No. Not really."

"How are the children?"

"Fine. Muzit and Senait are here with me."

"What about Ruth and Tamar?"

I might as well lay it all out right now, I thought. The burden was becoming too great for me. "They decided to stay behind and fight. We saw them off to Sahel in Keren."

There was a long pause at the other end of the line. "Well... well," he resumed. "There is nothing we can do about it.... you just continue on here with Muzit and Senait as soon as possible."

It was clear to me that Mesfun was disappointed despite the brave face he was putting on for me; on the other hand, I was relieved that the news had been broken to him at last.

Our little group of seasoned travelers dispersed in Port Sudan. Our cowardly male companion had a relative to go to; two of the girls hoped to locate a friend, even though they did not even have an address; while the other girl planned to proceed to Saudi Arabia to be with her sister, the mother of the child.

Little did we know that the worst of our travels was yet to come.

More unbearable even than the sordid experiences of Karora and Toker were the conditions aboard the third-class train that took us from Port Sudan to Khartoum — a journey of two days and one night. The children and I had only one seat for the three of us, and beside us sat a sick woman who kept throwing up. A *tegadalai* who was going to Khartoum on a mission accompanied us and was quite willing to stand the whole time; only at my insistence did he finally agree to take my seat for occasional short spells. The aisle of the train was packed with passengers and their belongings, which included even live chickens, and the various smells did nothing to help matters.

I could see in the eyes of my children their longing for the comforts of home.

We arrived in the Kober section of Khartoum in the middle of the night and took a taxi to EPLF headquarters, which was also used as accommodations.

"*Merhaba*" — welcome, said the *tegadalai* who opened the gate, rubbing his eyes. He led us to the kitchen and we spoke for a few minutes before he and I recognized each other. It was

Chimar, a relative who would occasionally come to our house when I was a girl of fourteen or fifteen. My children and I were exhausted from the arduous train trip, but we felt at home at EPLF headquarters in the company of an hospitable relative. Although my little ones and I could hardly keep our eyes open, Chimar insisted that we have something to eat before turning in. There was *engera* with *zigni*, and then we took our places on the floor of a large room where five other people were already sleeping. Neither my daughters nor I felt the mosquito bites, and by then we had become used to sleeping on a hard floor.

# Fifteen

My children and I spent three weeks in the sweltering heat of dusty Khartoum, a city swarming with mosquitoes and teeming with refugees from many parts of war-torn Africa.

As they were the only two children, at the time, among the many adults of the Kober EPLF family, much was made of Muzit and Senait. Visitors to the EPLF center would take them to downtown Khartoum and treat them to cakes and ice cream.

Most of the *tegadelti* I had seen in Keren were young, but many of those I met in Khartoum were my contemporaries, and some were well into middle age. My very first morning I was overjoyed to wake up and see that among the many bodies sharing the floor of the Kober EPLF premises with us was a colleague from the Relief and Rehabilitation Association for Eritrea. Dr. Teklemariam Zego had been head of the research committee in Asmara and was now a committed fighter with the department of agriculture. I also ran into Dr. Andom Ogba, who had been chair of our Sahel branch in Afabet and was now a *tegadalai* posted to the Orota Hospital in Sahel. Their work brought these two men to Khartoum frequently and it was a thrill to be able to reminisce about the days when we had worked together as a team.

It was in Khartoum that I saw and felt the whole panorama of our suffering — we the Eritrean people — from wounded fighters to refugee families. There were many families living in one-room houses with no toilet or running water. Over vast areas outside Khartoum, refugees from Eritrea, Ethiopia, and Sudan's other neighbors torn apart by war passed their days in devastating conditions, trying to protect themselves and their families from the scorching sun with whatever scraps of cardboard or tin they could find. Children were born and died in the hostile environment of these refugee camps. One could not help but be overcome by a sense of futility at the sight of these human castaways. It became very clear to me in Khartoum that when people are forced to live away from their homeland, most of the time they become demoralized and retreat into helplessness.

Zeggai was a farmer before he joined the EPLF. He was twenty-four years old and had a wife and two children. During the battle of Mai Atal, near Massawa, he had been a victim of a Soviet weapon that disperses fragments throughout the body and cannot be detected on X-ray. Zeggai, suffered excruciating pain in his thighs; when it became unbearable he would close his eyes, purse his lips, and shake his head violently from side to side. When his pain eased a little, I would try to distract him by telling him about America: not about the skyscrapers, the bridges, the theaters, the museums, but about the vast agricultural lands, the miles and miles of wheatfields and cornfields that I had seen in 1968 while driving to Chicago through Indiana. Born and raised in the countryside, Zeggai's ultimate dream was an Eritrea where he could plow his land free from the harassment, mining, and bombardment of the enemy! His immediate goal, however, despite his suffering, was to recover and return to combat.

The arrival from the field of a badly wounded *tegadalai* sent Kober into a deathly silence. Afeworki had been wounded in the head, and his face was unrecognizable due to extreme swelling. He was in a coma when he was brought from Sahel by truck. We prepared a bed for him in Zeggai's room. His nurse, Alem, administered Afeworki's intravenous and his injections, bathed him, and washed his clothes. He ate very little and slept on the floor beside Afeworki's bed.

In the morning Alem got up while the rest of us were still sleeping and he nursed Afeworki. Then he put on a pair of coveralls and spent some hours working on a small EPLF car. Alem was a nurse, a truck driver, and a skilled mechanic! I was amazed, but after three weeks at the Kober EPLF facility in Khartoum I would come to realize that Alem's case was not unique; this kind of versatility and dedication were trademarks of our *tegadelti*.

I did not want Muzit and Senait to be exposed to the sight of Afeworki, but I found that they could not remain sheltered forever from the cruel effects of war.

Just before dawn on the third day after his arrival, while the papers were being processed so that he could be sent to Rome for further treatment, Afeworki passed away. He was barely twenty-eight years old. I last saw him at midnight, before retiring for the night to the roof with my children and the other visitors. There were fewer mosquitoes on the balconied roof, and it was soothing to sleep in the open air. Next morning I left my children sleeping soundly and descended the stairs. About ten people normally slept in the large room downstairs but now there was no one. The place looked grim. I walked to Zeggai and Afeworki's room. Afeworki's bed was empty, and when Zeggai failed to answer when I said "Good morning," I knew that death had visited in the night.

Adanesh, who volunteered with the housekeeping while she was waiting to emigrate to Saudi Arabia, began to cry when she saw me coming into the kitchen. "When will the burial be?" I asked, weeping.

"There is no ceremony here. It is just as it is in the field. They have already gone to bury him."

I tried to be cheerful around my children, but the EPLF family in Kober mourned silently for three days in Afeworki's honor.

Muzit and Senait kept pestering me with questions about when they were finally going to see my brother Paulos. As head of the Eritrean Relief Association (ERA), Paulos lived in Khartoum but he was away on a mission when we arrived. A week after our arrival, Paulos returned to Khartoum. Even though my shock had lasted only a second when the Major at the Palace Prison had said that the sword of the Dergue could reach all the way to Paulos in the United States, I nevertheless felt relieved and overjoyed to see him standing in the flesh right there before my eyes.

I invited Paulos to a restaurant for dinner. After dinner we went to the terrace and reminisced about the days before our family had been torn apart. I had not seen him in five years; since he left home to study law in the United States as a post-graduate. Muzit remembered flying with Mesfun and my parents to attend his graduation from Haile Selassie University in Addis Ababa when she was five years old; but Senait could hardly be expected to remember Paulos patiently waiting with his camera to capture her very first few faltering steps.

I shared with him the trying period when *Abboi*, Mesfun, and I had all been in prison, and I recounted my flight from Addis Ababa, our perilous journey out of Asmara, and how I had felt when Ruth and Tamar told me about their decision to join the EPLF.

Muzit and Senait played freely, while Paulos spoke at length of what had made him suspend his studies and join the struggle. He recountered a sad story from 1970-71, when he had been a legal adviser to the Confederation of Ethiopian Labor Unions in Asmara. The case involved the Italian-owned Salina Massawa salt factory in the port of Massawa. The factory employed a large number of hired employees, and paid them poorly. Not only did the intense heat of Massawa and the reflection of the sun upon the white salt sap the energy of the workers, but the glare would often cause them to go blind. The employees had no benefits whatsoever, since their jobs were considered seasonal; even though some of them had worked for the company for as long as thirty years. The work consisted of trapping sea water in a pond and letting it evaporate to turn into salt. The salt is then removed and the pond is cleaned for the same process. The evaporation takes a few weeks. Then the workers would be laid off, their "contracts" terminated; they would be hired again as "new" employees.

The case of one Salina Massawa worker in particular was striking to Paulos. Having worked all his life for a meager salary, already clinically blind from the glare of the sun, this man's plea to Paulos was not that he be compensated for his disability but that management be pressed into replacing him with his son: that his son be sentenced to a lifetime of drudgery only to end his days blind like his father. The man knew no other life; there were no choices open to him. Management refused his plea. Such are the hidden injustices inflicted upon our people as a result of colonization and foreign ownership, whether British, Italian, or Ethiopian, Paulos said, and he felt that such injustices must be stopped.

"When you and I were growing up, the number of well-off Eritreans was very small. My dream for an independent Eritrea is for everyone to be prosperous and happy. That for me is what the struggle is all about," Paulos said as we stood to leave the restaurant.

Sleeping on the roof of the EPLF premises, my two children at either side, facing the moon and the stars, the awesome beauty of the blue Nile below us shimmering under the streetlights, gave me great comfort; meeting my brother Paulos and many old friends gave me much joy; tending our wounded fighters, even if briefly, gave me a sense of fulfilment. But seeing the intolerable conditions under which our people were forced to live, hearing about the human suffering, witnessing the death of a young hero: the combined trauma of Khartoum and being separated from my daughters would haunt me for quite some time.

Many friends from the Eritrean Relief Association and from the EPLF office saw us off at the airport in Khartoum, and Muzit and Senait were unhappy having to say goodbye to their uncle and the wonderful people who had been spoiling them.

"Please don't worry about Ruth and Tamar, Abeba — they will be fine," said Paulos as we were leaving. "They are a credit to the family. Continue the fight from Washington, as you and Mesfun planned it. The girls will be happy just knowing that you are both committed."

We left Sudan and flew to England on the eighth of March 1978, and what a stark contrast between hot, dry, sunny Khartoum and cold, damp, foggy London! I had gone to school during the British régime in Eritrea and had read many English novels. Despite my resentment of the British Regime, on my very first visit to England in the 1960s I fell in love with London; it had been then and still was the home of many of our friends and colleagues, and now it was also refuge for my brothers Petros and Solomon.

It was wonderful to see Petros well and fully committed to the EPLF and not, as my interrogators had hoped, captured in battle and in the hands of the Dergue's thugs. The news of my incarceration was exceptionally painful to Solomon. He was afraid I might be sentenced to 10-15 years or even get killed. He even temporarily suspended his studies in leather technology at Northapmton for lack of concentration. He was flabbergasted when he saw the three of us at Heathrow Airport

Muzit and Senait told their uncles about their experiences in Khartoum, and how their sisters had left us in Keren. Although he was living in London, Petros was a *tegadalai* and he was clearly proud of Ruth and Tamar. Solomon was full of admiration for them too, but I could see that he was a little worried. In that one-room apartment, clustered together on the floor around the gas heater after dinner, my brothers and I talked over old times.

When Petros, had temporarily come to live with Mesfun and I in 1975, we had agreed that he would call whenever he did not expect to be home for lunch. On the third of March he neither telephoned nor came home, and I was very worried. At four in the afternoon his best friend, Alem Ghedei, called me at my office to ask if I had heard from Petros. This only worsened my anxiety, for if anyone would know of Petros' whereabouts it was Alem. Then Alem came to my office and told me the sad news about the death of two *tegadelti*, Andom and Yemane, who had come to town from the field to coordinate the collection of medical supplies. The secret police had been tipped off about the meeting , and the house was immediately surrounded by *afagn*. There was no way out for Andom and Yemane: they burned the documents they had with them and took a gun to their own heads.

Meanwhile, Amahatzion and Russom, friends of Petros and Alem, had been seen driving the *tegadelti* to the meeting place. Russom made it to the field, but the unfortunate Amahatzion was caught. Petros was a member of the same cell, so he left Asmara immediately. All this happened at eleven o'clock in the morning, and Petros was out of the city before noon, we would later learn.

That particular afternoon, Lia answered the telephone and heard a simple message "Petros is okay" and nothing more. *Abboi* refused to believe the message. In the morning he drove to our house but refused to get out of the car and come in. He said not a word for several moments; he just sat staring straight ahead into the distance, his face as lifeless as a stone. Finally forcing himself to speak, he asked if I would go with him to the morgue — where we might be lucky enough to find Petros' body. "How would I break the news to your mother?" He lamented. "Whether Petros' body is found or not, it would be unbearable for her." I have seen my father in many agonizing circumstances, but never have I seen him so immobilized with grief, with the exception of the morning he bade me goodbye at the Palace prison grounds.

Now, as we sat in London, my brothers wanted to know

not only about the reaction of our parents to Petros' sudden disappearance, but the story of my own imprisonment. Petros laughed when I told him that during my interrogation I denied that we were very close as brother and sister. I had taken the advice of my cellmates at the *ghebi* prison — that the name of the game was deny, deny, deny, even if they crucified one.

There was anger in his voice, though, when Petros told me that it was impossible for the EPLF to approach the British government as Eritreans. The United Kingdom honored the myth of Ethiopian territorial integrity to the letter, refusing to so much as acknowledge Eritrea's legitimacy even as ratified by the United Nations. We also talked at length about the fear of Russian involvement in the Ethio-Eritrean war, which was the subject of conversation whenever two or more Eritreans gathered.

I was amazed that a person who loved the good life as much as Petros, had been willing to change his lifestyle in order to serve his country. A *tegadalai* or a *tegadalit* lives like one whether he or she is living in Eritrea or abroad. Both Petros and Solomon were content to sleep on the floor, leaving the beds for Muzit, Senait, and myself. They had forsaken all comforts anyway.

Solomon's dream was to return home and modernise *Abboi's* business, but like every Eritrean he had to temporarily halt his plans. He would later be hired by an American tanning factory in Haiti. In all of Solomon's letters to me from that faraway land, he would plead for information on the Eritrean struggle: any acknowledgement at the United Nations; an encouraging newspaper article; some direct news from home.

When I was in Haz Haz, Mesfum had told me that friends all over were praying for me. Some of these friends were members of Moral Re-Armament: people like the Elliotts, the Smiths, Joy Weeks, and Heather Hopecraft, to mention a few. The Smiths and the Elliotts had worked in Asmara for a few years, both couples returning to England in the mid-1970s, not too long before I was imprisoned. I now found Bridget Elliot to be partially paralyzed and speech-impaired, yet her spirit was extraordinary. I spent some wonderful times with my old friends in London and Oxford on this visit to England.

Muzit, Senait, and I flew the last leg of our journey, from London to Washington, on the nineteenth of March 1978. It was a great moment for all of us when we were reunited with Mesfun! It was three months since I had fled Addis Ababa and set in motion our circuitous journey to the United States, and it was more than four months since Mesfun had left, ostensibly to attend the seminar in Nairobi and then return. The children and I felt very sad arriving without Ruth and Tamar, however; and their decision to stay behind struck Mesfun, I think, only when he was confronted at the airport with the reality. My two teenagers left a terrible void in our family that never would quite heal.

Two of my younger sisters who lived in Houston, came to Washington with their husbands to see us. Six years had passed since my sisters had left for the United States; I was happy to see that not only had they both matured in the intervening years, they had become ardently committed to the cause of a free Eritrea. Demekesh and her husband, Mengesteab Worede, and Medhin with her husband, Haile Tecle, were all staunch members of the Eritrean Students' Association in North America, a mass organisation of the EPLF. This meeting in Washington was one of the most touching moments of all our lives.

# Sixteen

Most Eritreans in exile felt that independence was at hand. Ninety-five per cent of Eritrea was liberated; only the ports of Massawa and Assab remained. Asmara was under siege. Yet all of us harbored an unspoken fear. Why are the Russians suddenly befriending Ethiopia? Why is the Ethiopian civilian airline busy transporting soldiers and Russian weapons to Eritrea? What is the mission of the Russian Antonovs flying back and forth between Asmara and Addis? We had thought the Soviet Union would never actually become fully involved, would never deploy personnel and armaments for the purpose of annihilating three and a half million human beings. What about the Soviet Union's suport for Eritrean independence in the 1950s?

But the long-feared involvement of the Soviet Union on the side of Ethiopia against Eritrea did become reality. The role of the Russians changed: They were no longer advising, supplying weapons, and training troops; they were now planning and directing a major offensive.

One morning in November 1978 I opened our front door and there on our doormat lay the *Washington Post* — and on the front page was a headline declaring that Keren had fallen to the Ethiopians and that the Eritrean "rebels" had been wiped out.

Bombs had rained down on Eritrean-controlled civilian areas with an intensity unprecedented in the history of our armed struggle. Thousands of innocent people were massacred, countless numbers of domestic animals were slaughtered, and crops and property were destroyed. A great many people who had been spared from death were left to suffer from the effects of incendiary and anti-personnel bombs. The ELF took irreversible losses. The EPLF had to withdraw from the cities and towns to their base area in Sahel; but they had not been decimated, as the newspapers were reporting.

In the face of such a huge army with all their deadly weapons, the EPLF made the right decision in retreating, for they could come back with renewed zeal and better tactics. But it was a bitter pill for us all to swallow. They would have to go from almost total success back to square one and recapture villages, towns, and cities. The human loss and suffering that this would entail was appalling.

I was broken-hearted by the indifference of the United Nations; I could not understand the spinelessness of the members of the Organization for African Unity. To the Eastern bloc we were considered tools of the West, the Arabs, and imperialism. To the West we were Marxists. No one saw us simply as "people." Among the very few international journalists, there was only one American, to my knowledge, who was trying to bring to light the injustice and horror of what was going on in our faraway belea-guered homeland, the freelance writer Don Connell.

Mesfun had worked for the U.S. government in various capacities at home, and with many friends in the State Department, we were confident that the two of us would be unof-ficial ambassadors for Eritrea. It did not take us long to discover, however, that getting through to the State Department and the United Nations without the benefit of a political machine and a fully-equipped lobbying office was like trying to push through a wall with bare hands.

There was nothing we could do but contribute money to the struggle through the Eritrean Students' Association in North America, and soon after the offensive had begun, I fell into a state of despair.

I should have stayed and suffered with my people, I thought, rather than come abroad to live a life of utter futility. I had nightmares about the horror of prison life. I was haunted by the image of countless people buried in mass graves

I had a recurring dream: I was walking along the stream that ran near our apartment in Virginia, and the sound of the clear, babbling water would begin to relax me. Then I would hear Tamar's voice: "Mommy, Mommy." I would try to follow the sound of the voice but was never able to trace it. I would see Tamar as an eight-year-old, in her green and white striped Sunday dress, her long hair done up in two braids. Tamar would be trapped somewhere in the stream, and I would look for her. But her voice would become fainter and fainter until eventually I would cease to hear anything at all.

"Tamar, where are you. Please talk to me," I would call out in desperation. Then I always woke up in a cold sweat, my heart pounding. The nightmare lasted several weeks and it got so real that I did not want to go to bed at all.

One Saturday afternoon I went to the actual stream and sat for almost an hour on a rock, hoping to hear Tamar's voice. Then my own actions began to scare me, and I started to make my way home. And this time I was convinced I heard her voice. Tamar's "Mommy, Mommy" had become familiar to me, even in broad daylight.

I heard the same calling another time while I was walking on a busy street. I went to a darkened parking lot where I would not be seen and I cried my heart out. The idea of Tamar's being wounded and trapped in battle somewhere constantly haunted me.

With all these nightmares and the mental turmoil that had become my constant companion, I knew that I had to do something or else lose my mind. I was afraid to open letters or answer the telephone because of what I might read or hear about Ruth or Tamar. We heard that my sister Lia had joined the front. I feared what I might hear about Lia, the baby of the family.

Back home, people go to what are considered holy places to be cured of their illnesses and to gain inner strength and peace. There are many such places throughout Eritrea; in Asmara, people bathe for seven or fourteen days in the holy waters of St. Mary, St. Michael, or St. Gaber, and accompany the bathing with prayer and fasting. I decided that I would make do with the ordinary bath water of our American apartment. I bathed for seven consecutive days at a certain time — forty-five minutes early in the morning — visualizing the entire time that I was being healed. The fear of getting up and facing the day began to diminish. There were still moments when I felt morbid, but over time these became fewer and less intense. My depression was finally under control.

Our original idea of emigrating to the United States had been to help the motherland: to join other Eritreans in making the

West aware of the tragic situation of our people; to prick the conscience of the United Nations. Many of us were still wondering how to go about our mission when Operation Red Star began in October 1981.

More than two years had passed since our *tegadelti* had withdrawn to their base in Sahel. The Dergue were fearful and suspicious of what the EPLF were up to.

"Once and for all, we shall obliterate the "rebels" who are hindering economic development in Eritrea; and any Eritrean parents who stand by their sons and daughters shall be exterminated. The government cannot be disrupted by a bunch of bandits." So said the Ethiopian leader, Mengistu Hailemariam, as he addressed his officials during preparations for the famous Operation Red Star offensive.

Mengistu literally transferred his office from Addis Ababa to Asmara for this offensive, and his army of two hundred and fifty thousand soldiers was augmented by a contingent of specialists and a dazzling array of hardware from the Eastern bloc.

An Eritrean woman who had come from Asmara to Washington to visit her children at that time told us that for a whole month an ominous shadow hung over Asmara: Russian planes bringing soldiers from Addis Ababa; helicopters hovering over the city; tanks roaring up and down the main streets. The Russian presence had become more obvious than ever, and that the people were being bombarded with incessant propaganda. The EPLF kept telling the public over their Sahel radio station — which the Russians had not been able to jam — not to panic, to stay calm. They seemed to be prepared for anything.

Just as the streets of Asmara were packed with strangers, the woman reported, so were the mosques and the churches filled to overflowing. The three main Christian denominations — Orthodox, Catholic, and Protestant — worshipped together at the different churches by rotation. People settled their differences and made peace. Mothers prayed for their children.

Mengistu was joined in this offensive by the Russians, the East Germans, the Cubans, the South Yemenis, and the Libyans. The Soviet Union contributed billions of dollars in arms, along with three thousand Soviet advisers, generals, and specialists. East Germany took over Ethiopian security completely. Castro's troops, sixteen thousand strong, patrolled the Somali border so that the Ethiopian Third Division posted there would be free to participate in the battle. South Yemenis were assigned as pilots and tank drivers. Gadaffi made his oil money available.

The West, for its part, had apparently severed relations with Mengistu's Ethiopia because of its human rights violations; yet they gave him covert and overt economic aid, which more often than not went to feed his colossal army.

And who rallied to the side of Eritrea in the face of this unholy alliance? Almost no one. Forget military support — the EPLF had always had only the weapons they captured in battle — but even the meager humanitarian aid to Eritrea now stopped. The only help came from Eritreans — those still living in terror inside Eritrea and those vast numbers of us living in exile — scattered by the four winds to every corner of the globe.

Mengistu's intensive war propaganda — blaming all of Ethiopia's ills on the *tegadelti*, had achieved the desired result. The world speculated that indeed the Eritrean people would be crushed once and for all; and what country would want to be on the side of the loser?

"The planes, tanks, and armored cars would be effective if the *tegadelti* were fighting in cities and towns," said Mesfun. "But deploying all this machinery in mountainous Sahel, against our dedicated EPLF: It will not work. Moreover, it will not be easy to move such a big army."

What Mesfun said made sense, but I was still worried. "You are right," I offered half-heartedly. "This may be the beginning of the end for the Dergue."

Indeed it proved to be the beginning of their demise. The much publicized Operation Red Star was a total failure.

In pursuing their dream of keeping Eritrea under Ethiopian control, the Dergue not only exposed its own people to sickness, famine, and poverty, but it was confronted with civil war on its own soil. The Tigreans, who had long been neglected and downtrodden, took up arms in 1975, proved to be highly organized, and became a real threat to Mengistu. After the Tigrai People's Liberation Front (TPLF) was formed, several other antigovernment organizations had sprung up and the Dergue had to fight on many fronts.

# Seventeen

There was no direct mail service to liberated Eritrea. Most letters went via the Eritrean Relief Association in Khartoum. Moreover, *tegadelti* changed posts as the need arose, so delays in receiving mail from fighters and getting letters to them was expected.

It was therefore some months after Ruth was married in 1980 that we finally received word; and several months after Tamar's marriage the following year that we received her joyous letter. Then, on the twenty-fifth of February 1985, Tamar gave birth to a baby boy. When we heard about this great event, all four of us had ambivalent feelings. We were happy that a child had been born into our family, making grandparents of Mesfun and I, and aunts of Muzit and Senait; yet we were uneasy because we knew how incredibly difficult it is to bring up a child where death and destruction are part of life, where everybody is overworked, and where food and clothing are in short supply.

"What is here for children but the constant fear of aerial bombardment, malnutrition, and misery," wrote Tamar, eight months after her baby had been born. "I cannot give my child what you and Papa gave me, and I refuse to abandon the cause that I have defended for eight years. I would be the happiest mother in the world if you would agree to raise my son until freedom has been achieved. I would be indebted to you for the rest of my life, Mommy. Given the choice, I would much rather raise Eskinder myself, especially during his tender years. But I'm afraid I have to put my maternal instincts aside for now and think of his welfare. I love you, Mommy, and I hope to receive a positive reply."

Tamar's letter hit me like a ton of bricks. This did not look at all feasible; I was in no position to raise a small child. I decided the only way to tell Tamar would be to go to Eritrea and explain the situation in person. I had longed to return and see her, Ruth, my youngest sister Lia, and all the heroic fighters long before Tamar's baby had come along, but somehow the trip had never materialized.

I stuffed my suitcases with shirts, pants, underwear, and all kinds of small necessities that one would never normally think of as gifts — needles and thread, scissors, mirrors, combs — and on the sixteenth of June 1986 I flew to Khartoum via London. It was ten p.m. when we arrived in Khartoum, and the African airport with its soft evening breeze was for me a real treat. It was wonderful to be under the African sky after eight years away — it was even marvelous to be in dusty Khartoum.

Like most other visitors, I went to the Eritrean Relief Association offices before proceeding to the field. I found the ERA offices completely transformed since I had been in Khartoum in February 1978. They had been moved to far more spacious premises in the center of the city, and looked quite modern with the typewriters and computers. The offices were bustling with activity.

Paulos told me that since the 1984-85 Ethiopian-Eritrean drought had captured the attention of the world, much-needed aid had been pouring in. While Ethiopia got the lion's share of the relief, the funds flowing in to Eritrea were significant enough to make a dent. As I sat in the ERA's waiting room, I marveled at the variety and scope of the programmes that the organization was undertaking, not only in relief but also in rehabilitation and development. The ERA water development program had begun in 1981 with a few technicians digging wells with rudimentary tools; now they were well on the way to benefitting hundreds of thousands of people, minimizing the constant shortages and providing clean drinking water in rural areas. Poor farmers were being given the means to remain on the land. Conservation and reforestation programs had been launched, a technical school had been opened, supplementary food for schoolchildren was being produced. Donor agencies marveled at how efficiently ERA handled relief supplies and implemented its programs.

The first old friend I met in the ERA offices was Tekie Beyene. We talked at length about the war, the famine, and his relief work. I filled him in on our decision to flee Addis Ababa for the West, and about how torn I had been when my daughters joined the front. Tekie's own decision to leave his wife and children behind to join first the EPLF and then ERA was not easy. Toward the end of our conversation, his mood changed, and looking off into the distance, as if he were talking to himself, he said: "But I had to make a choice. Had I continued to work at the bank and yet remain heavily involved with the EPLF, it was evident that sooner or later I would be killed or arrested. And what good would I have been dead or in prison? Here, I am serving my motherland — which means working towards the creation of a better place for my children. My wife and I share a deep understanding. We had learned long before to always take the rough with the smooth." Tekie's eyes misted over. "Sometimes, I must confess, I feel that I deserted her — she who is my life — and the wonderful children she bore me. But I was compelled to leave. I had to."

Then I talked at length with Nura Mohammed. Although Nura and I had once worked for the same airline, our close relationship was formed through the YWCA. We used to have great times during Christmas celebrations and other get-togethers at the YWCA.

"Nura," I said, "it must be wonderful for you to have a child!" Her daughter, Sara, was then about four.

"Oh, it is great," she said. "Only I'm so busy in the office, I cannot give her much attention. Mother finally managed to get out of Asmara and she is helping me with Sara. I should be thankful for that, but..." Her voice trailed off for an instant. "But I have a hard time explaining why her father cannot be with us all the time." For the first time, I noticed that there were fine lines under her eyes.

"Sara and I went to Sahel to see Ibrahim, and we stayed two months." Nura said. Sara became more restless when we returned to Sudan; she really misses her father.... It has been a year now since I've heard from him." Tears welled up in Nura's eyes, but as a dedicated *tegaladit* she did not want to show any sign of weakness. I would later learn that Ibrahim, an EPLF veteran and a military commander, was killed by an enemy bullet.

Every Eritrean, whether still under direct control of the Ethiopian government, living in the liberated area, or living abroad, has a unique but always painful story to tell, and one learns early on to avoid asking certain questions. There were some aspects of my own life that I did not like to discuss. I felt as though I had one foot in cold water and the other in hot. Two of my daughters were living in safety but away from their homeland, deprived of their grandparents, their sisters, and the family support system; and two were battling the enemy, their lives constantly in danger.

Just as I was stepping out of the ERA offices, I ran into Dr. Assefaw Tekeste, who had arrived from the field the previous night; doctors from the liberated areas would occasionally travel to Sudan or Europe to attend medical conferences. We had a very brief but pleasant time reminiscing about our few turbulent yet rewarding months working together as volunteers with the Relief and Rehabilitation Association for Eritrea. I told Dr. Assefaw of my concern when I had caught sight of him at the Palace Prison. I was afraid he would be interrogated and tortured over the matter of the three tractors seized by *tegadelti*.

The day before I was to fly to Port Sudan, I was happily surprised to run into another friend, Dr. Michael Gebre-Hiwot, at the ERA residence. Dr. Michael was a young surgeon who, with the cooperation of Catholic nuns, had clandestinely vaccinated and treated large numbers of rural children. Then when our relief association had been established, he joined us and worked openly and ceaselessly, going from village to village.

"People say the struggle has made great strides in medicine. How can this be, under such abominable conditions?" I asked Dr. Michael when we had finished dinner and everybody at the residence was relaxing after the hustle and bustle of the day.

"In a devastating war like ours, out of necessity you learn more quickly by practice than by going to school," he said. "So, yes, we have made strides. But this is not what one would call 'dramatic progress'"

Then he told me about how they would go to the countryside to teach modern techniques to the midwives and dispensers of folk medicine rather than dismiss them and discard their ways as outmoded. Small mud-hut clinics were being set up in villages and rural people were being taught basic hygiene They had to deal with terribly deficient diets and in their work they were constantly confronted with the effects of lack of fruits and vegetables. Drought and the war were always in the way.

"In the Eritrea of the future," said my former colleague,

"the money now spent on trying to run big hospitals in the cities will be put towards clinics in the villages, so that everybody will be able to benefit from the best that modern medicine has to offer But there is no reason for us not to keep the old tried and true practices as well."

After three days in hot, dry, Khartoum — the sun barely visible through the thick haze of brown dust — I flew to Port Sudan on the Red Sea Coast.

It was late afternoon when we arrived. I shared a taxi with another Eritrean from the airport to the rented house that served as the residence for the Eritrean Relief Association. I was welcomed by a young woman called Lula, who led me to one of the bedrooms and gestured for me to take any one of the four beds. The mosquitoes were neither as plentiful nor as persistent as they had been in Khartoum, but I nevertheless rubbed my hands and feet with mosquito repellent and curled up on the bed nearest the window. When I woke up dinner was ready.

There were eight of us that evening for dinner that consisted of lentil *tsebhi* with bread. Lula sat next to a man with an artificial leg which he removed in order to sit comfortably. Her eyes followed him when he stood and hopped into the kitchen for some water; and then, like a dutiful wife, she took the glass for him when he searched for a place for it on the table.

The next day, Lula told me that six weeks earlier she had come from Beirut, where she had been working for some years, to join the struggle. Upon her arrival in Port Sudan, she met an EPLF veteran whose job now was assembling artificial limbs.

"I came here to give myself to my country, and I was given this great gift — my man. We got married two weeks after my arrival. We have been together a month now."

"How are you going to feel leaving him behind when the time comes time for you to go to Sahel for training?" I asked Lula.

"I know there is a chance that I will never see him again, but there is no going back. I'll just have to make the most of the next two weeks," she said in a low voice, sounding a little unsure despite her show of bravado. "Tekeste is forever trying to tell me about how he would love to have children, but I always cut him short — I know how awful it would be for both of us." Lula was beginning to sound melancholy. She had no idea where she was going to be sent after basic training.

"Now that I have met the man of my dreams, I am torn: I still want to fight for my country, yet at the same time I love Tekeste and I want to bear his children." There were tears in her eyes. My heart went out to her. What a dilemma. In the history of our *tegadelti*, I thought, there must be a number of marriages like this: extraordinarily romantic, painful, and short. There was a very real chance that this couple would never meet again. Lula could very well be killed in battle, or she could develop a relationship with someone else — a person with whom she works closely on a daily basis.

The next day an old acquaintance who was also staying at ERA premises walked me to the paraplegic rehabilitation clinic, a three-story building funded by the Eritrean Relief Association, and introduced me to the head of the clinic. We chatted briefly in his office and then he gave me a tour. The paraplegics were largely men and boys. Some were asleep, some were in wheelchairs, and a few walked with the aid of crutches. The sight of one young man in his late twenties, is still vivid in my memory: He was in severe pain just venturing to take one small step with his new crutches, beads of perspiration visible across the bridge of his nose. Then I shook hands with a woman in a wheelchair, and she chatted easily about her situation. I wanted to talk to another veteran but he was too engrossed in his daily workout: I had to be content with his gracious smile as he carried on with his exercizes. One boy told me he had a cousin in America; he gave me the name and asked me if I knew him. "America is a big continent," I explained. "I don't know your cousin, but I could try to find out about him when I go back." The young man was obviously disappointed; it was beyond his comprehension that Eritreans could live in the same country and yet not know each other!

I gave the health officer of the clinic the token gifts that I had brought: two decks of playing cards, a dozen combs and nail clippers.

When I returned to the residence I found two Europeans in the living room talking with an ERA member, so I slipped unnoticed to the bedroom and lay on my bed staring at the ceiling. I tried to blot out the image of those paraplegics, war veterans between the tender ages of nineteen and twenty-five; instead of seeing the pathos of our young heroes, I tried to concentrate on the positive. They were affirming their existence and demonstrating their faith in the future by going through strenuous and excruciating therapy. They were so courageous and so very hopeful.

I returned to the living room to chat with the other guests. One of them was a Norwegian, a member of a church that had already given substantial help and was eager to do more. The other was a British student waiting for transportation to Sahel to learn about the curriculum at the Zero School, where, incidentally, my daughter Tamar was working. The Zero School was a boarding school that was founded in the liberated area in 1976 with ninety children, mostly orphans or children of fighters and nomads; the school's curriculum and its techniques had been attracting the attention of educators internationally in recent years.

Shortly after I had been introduced to these men, as I sat there trying to follow their conversation, who should show up but Haile! The ten years of war and hardship had left their mark on him, but his distinctive boyish smile was still there. Six years in combat had cost him neither an eye nor a limb, and he gave me the latest news of Ruth, Tamar, and Lia. He asked for information about his loved ones, but, unfortunately, I had nothing to tell. I later learned that he had been married for three years and that his wife had been killed in battle.

The next morning I met Askalu Menkarios, whom I had known in Asmara. She was now vice-chair of ERA. Askalu was a former Ethiopian Airlines employee, stationed in Addis Ababa, and the last I had seen of her was the day she had come to our house with Petros before she slipped away and joined the struggle in 1975. I also met Senai, her husband, who ran the pharmacy in Sahel and was now en route to Khartoum on an EPLF mission. Askalu was stationed in Khartoum but was often away from the city on relief matters. The wife and husband, and their two-year-old daughter, had a stolen moment of two whole days! In wartime Eritrea, such luxuries were at a premium.

At five o'clock in the afternoon of the third day, it was time for me to leave Port Sudan, along with three *tegadelti* and the British student. Lula and I said our reluctant goodbyes. We loaded our bags into the Toyota Land Cruiser and set out on the road to Suakin, where we would stay the night; we would be proceeding to Eritrea before dawn the next day.

The old forsaken port of Suakin is only an hour's drive from Port Sudan. The buildings must have been magnificent in Suakin's heyday. Even in ruins, the city looked ancient and majestic, in the yellowish-red glow of the sunset. The splendid sunset in Suakin made me think that one day, one day soon, we would be free from the bondage of war and all the evil that goes with it. Families would be reunited, and everyone would be at peace to enjoy nature.

The rehabilitation center in Suakin, was an extension of the clinic in Port Sudan. There were three large rooms and a big verandah, and beds had been placed both inside and out.

The driver, Germai, offered to take us to the EPLF garage before we retired for the night. An elderly, graceful Eritrean, who had been trained as a mechanic by the Italians in Asmara, proudly gave us a tour. I was amazed, for it did not look like a garage at all but a compound so huge that it looked like an entire port. But what was most staggering to me about the "garage" was the sight of women lifting and repairing heavy engines and other truck parts.

We set out at four the following morning with barely a word exchanged among us passengers. I was admiring Germai's driving skills — how he negotiated the rough dirt road in total darkness, without the benefit of anything as sophisticated as a road sign. The British youth did not seem to mind the bumpy ride; he had been a student in Egypt, and perhaps did not find the primitive conditions all that unusual. For my part, I was not as enthusiastic about seeing the sun rise as I normally would have been. My thoughts were with Ruth and Tamar. What was it going to be like seeing them in the flesh after eight long years? And what would my grandson look like? The photographs we had seen of him were taken when he was only three months old. Would I be lucky enough to see Lia?

We reached Kurbaraca at ten o'clock. There was an EPLF way station made up of tents which was erected under a big shaded tree. It had mud benches and was very cool and comfortable. Food and tea were served to travelers en route between Sahel and Sudan, and it also had a small garage for minor repairs. We stayed until the desert sun relented a little, and then it was back to the Land Cruiser.

As we were about to reach the border, I asked Germai to point it out to me. It was — nothing more than a stop sign and a small hut perched atop a cliff. When we got out of the car to show our papers and to register I looked up at the sky and knelt and kissed the ground. That stop sign in the middle of nowhere was a very special sight to me, and once we had crossed into Eritrea I felt refreshed and alert.

As the Toyota snaked its way along the winding road, we came upon a group of half-naked people washing their clothes in a stream. These were Ethiopian prisoners of war, Germai told me. I had always heard that the Ethiopian soldiers became more relaxed once they were captured. They were treated humanely and even taught to read and write. These were people whose own government, meanwhile, had disowned them; it did not negotiate for their release, nor did it attempt to open lines of communication with their captors. Even the renowned International Red Cross abandoned these unfortunate pawns in the struggle

The British student and I were Germai's only passengers now. "Would you prefer to go directly to Tamar's, or would you like to go to the guest house first?" he asked. I said I would rather go to the guest house so I could shower and change before she saw me. He dropped me at the guest house at six in the evening and said he would return soon to pick me up. "Soon" for me meant twenty to thirty minutes, but it was four hours that I waited for Germai to come for me. With the exception of my first night at the Palace Prison and the night Mesfum joined me as a prisoner, those were the longest four hours of my life.

While I was waiting for Germai, pacing back and forth to the window to see if he had arrived, I struck up a conversation with the director of the guest house. He knew Ruth and Tamar well. In fact, it was he who had met my two young patriots when the truck brought them to Sahel from Keren, after we had parted so sorrowfully in January 1978. Every *tegadalit* and *tegadalai* I met wanted to know whether their fellow Eritreans abroad were contributing their fair share financially and whether we were retaining our Eritrean culture, and this man was no exception. He also asked if Mesfum and I were giving our daughters the best possible edu cation so that they could help rebuild their homeland when the tim came.

Finally, at around half past ten, I heard a motor. My heart bega to race, knowing that in no time I would be with my daughter and m grandson. Germai was not in the car; it was Ghebremicael, the Eritrea Relief Association field coordinator, who would be taking me to Tamar'

The short distance to her place went very slowly, however. W kept stopping to pick up both children and adults, and the little car wa soon jammed with people. It was pitch black outside, the only light i the vast darkness coming from our headlights. Finally, after some twer ty minutes, the car came to a halt on a dried riverbed.

Ghebremicael pointed to a tiny twinkle of light on a nearby hil "That is where you will find Tamar," he said. It was hard to imagine tha people actually lived there. In Sahel, life begins at dusk and is in fu swing until the early hours of the morning, and Ghebremicael quickl unloaded my suitcases to go about his work.

The headlights soon disappeared completely, and the stars in th vast sky were too far away to be of much use. I found myself immob lized; I could budge not an inch from the spot where the car had left m A young boy whose face I could not see was standing beside me.

"Would you be kind enough to see if Tamar is really there?" asked.

"I know she is there, and Eskinder too," he replied.

"Okay, then. Please, tell her that somebody from America is her to see her. And if she asks who it is, tell her you think it might be he mother."

The boy climbed like a rabbit, only to come back and say tha Tamar did not believe him.

My heart became heavier and heavier as I started to climb th cliff. My knees were trembling. Where was my daughter? I had been s excited and so hopeful, and now suddenly I was completely drained. was so steep that I had to ask one of the boys to take my hand and pu me up. With every step my heart was pounding more and more. I wa worried that I would not even be able to make it up the hill to the litt hut where my daughter supposedly was.

If Tamar was really there, would she not come out to greet me Maybe something has happened since we last heard from her. I was cor sumed with terror.

The walk to the top of the hill seemed even longer than the hou

I had waited at the guest house. But once I made it, I took a deep breath and proceeded without the boy's help. Ten short steps, and I was at the entrance of the doorless hut.

I looked straight ahead. All I saw was black round shadows clustered together. My limbs betrayed me by shaking violently.

I saw two women sitting on a mud bench.

Then I saw two familiar eyes.

The next thing I knew we were embracing, our tears mingling. Tears of anguish and tears of joy. Eskinder was there, and when he saw his mother and a stranger weeping together, he started crying too.

What I had seen from the door was a group of *tegadelti* eating from one big plate; all that I had been able to discern in the dark hut was their heads. The young boys who had helped me were students from the Zero School — their safe time to play outside was at night, in the dark; they knew the lay of the land intimately.

Tamar had not taken the boy seriously, and had not believed it was me standing in the doorway of the hut until I turned my head towards her.

Skin and bones though she was, Tamar was alive!

During those first few minutes, not a word was to be heard from the group of people. My hands and Tamar's locked together, and we simply kept silent. Eskinder finally stopped crying and sat on a *tegadalai's* lap staring at us. It was hard for me to believe that that child was my grandson.

The five *tegadelti* took leave slowly, one by one, after we shook hands and exchanged greetings. Sertzu, Eskinder's father, Tamar, Eskinder, and I were left alone. A moment of quiet. The wind became harsh.

In my mind I went back to Tamar's childhood: how jolly and beautiful she was; how she enjoyed celebrating her birthday; how she loved to sing "Sonei Kustonei" and "Amazing Grace." What a stark difference between the circumstances of her childhood and those under which her son, my grandchild, was being brought up.

I am not going to be sentimental about it, I told myself. Whatever the circumstances, we are together, and that is all that counts. When I raised my head to shake the past from my mind, I noticed that Tamar was also deep in thought.

Tamar was a nurse at the Zero School. The three of them were on a two-week vacation, and they had been given the privacy of the hut, which had only recently been built to serve such a purpose. The several *tegadelti*, I learned, had merely stopped by to say hello, and since dinner was ready they had been invited to share it.

I had brought two bedsheets with me, and after midnight Tamar put blankets on the mud bed. Eskinder and his father slept on the floor. Tamar and I retired to the bed to talk. She was as caring as ever, doing her best to make the bed comfortable for me.

The wind grew more persistent now, spitting sand against the blanket that Sertzu had placed over the open doorway, and eventually becoming so violent that it ripped the blanket and sent sand flying into our hut. Amazingly, Eskinder slept soundly, and Tamar herself seemed to consider these conditions nothing out of the ordinary. She was worried about me, however, and she held me fast. It is true that there are times in our lives when our children mother us, and this was definitely one of those times.

Towards dawn, finally, the wind subsided, and after the chaos of the night the world seemed serene and fresh. Tamar apologized for the terrible night as though it had been her fault. Eskinder started the morning by crying. "In the space of just ten days," his mother said, "he has had two attacks of diarrhea."

Tamar sent a message to Ruth. "I have to warn you, though: The chances of Lia being able to get here are really remote," she said.

"Well, who knows? Word was sent to her group leader back when I was in Port Sudan." I was ever hopeful.

"Still, it takes time, Mommy. She is behind enemy lines, after all."

I knew in my heart of hearts that in all likelihood I would not be seeing Lia. I had once planned to bring her to the United States with us, but she had joined the EPLF. It would be wonderful, I thought, for us to have the chance to talk as adults. The age gap between us was so great that I felt I hardly knew my own sister.

Breakfast was tea with bread. I had brought along cheese

and jam. The cheese was for myself, since I had to be careful with my diet in order to avoid a flare-up of my gastritis; but when I saw Eskinder devouring it with the jam on his ration of bread I decided to throw caution to the wind and let him have it all. I would make do with the bread.

Tamar swept and tidied up the little seven-by-eight-foot hut — a typical village hut, with mud beds built into the three corners. The clothing and blankets were kept in plastic bags. There was also the ubiquitous portable radio.

Sertzu took Eskinder to visit in the neighborhood so that Tamar and I could have a few precious moments alone together.

"Well, let's go right back to the very beginning!" I said, "What happened after we said goodbye in Keren? How on earth did you survive the training?" We sat nestled to each other. "Tell me about all the hardships... and, Tamar, I want to know about the circumstances of your being injured, and losing your eyesight."

Not only had Ruth and Tamar managed to survive the training under the burning sun — they even surpassed some of the youths whose lives had been less sheltered than their own. Tamar gave me such wonderful details of their strenuous training and her life as a *tegadalit* that I felt I had walked with her through it. She clearly was not ready, though, to tell me about how she had been wounded. *Tegadelti* started dropping by, leaving no more time for intimacy.

Most of the visitors were young; very few could have been more than thirty. Almost all were disabled, and these *tegadelti* continued their commitment to the cause as teachers or as houseparents to children who had been orphaned or whose parents were at the front.

Eskinder and Sertzu returned late in the afternoon after having had their lunch of *engera* and *tsebhi* at the school cafeteria.

I spent the next two days attempting to establish a relationship with my grandson. Since I was afraid of an upset stomach, I was stuck with bread and chlorinated water. I was very hungry, but I reasoned that it would be better to starve than to get sick; in any case, I seemed to be fairly strong.

Tamar did not give me a chance to explain why I was not able to raise Eskinder. She told me that on second thought she regretted having written that letter. "I wasn't thinking objectively at the time. I just wanted the best for my child, but then I realized it could not possibly be that simple for you either. Anyway, I've decided that I want him with me, no matter what. I'm sorry, Mommy. But it's wonderful to have you here anyway!"

My main worry was Ruth. "Do you think she's alright?" I asked, trying without much success to hide my concern.

"Don't worry. Just in case the first message didn't reach her — which I'm sure it did — I sent a second one through someone I know very well, so there's no question that she'll get it."

I had no choice but to sit tight and wait.

I had lively conversations with many of the *tegadelti* who came to visit, but I remember two women in particular. They had both been wounded. One of them had lost a leg, and the other woman had lost an eye. They seemed to be well educated and both had read the books that I had written in Tigrinya in the 1970s.

"How do you find the field?" asked Manna, the woman with the artificial leg. "Here, in our remote little corner of Africa, we think of Dallas, Texas [where I was living at that time], as one huge ranch, full of cowboys."

There was a frightening number of disabled tegadelti, but I knew that I was seeing so many of them here because they staffed the underground schools, workshops, garages, and hospitals. There is no waste of manpower in the EPLF. I was still shocked each time I met yet one more veteran who was maimed or missing a limb or an eye — for the most part young men and women in their twenties and early thirties.

As I looked at Dehab, I could not keep from imagining how beautiful she must have been before she had lost her eye; it was now just an empty socket.

"When did you pay your dues to the homeland?" I asked both women.

*Tegadelti* learn early on to accord little or no importance to their own personal hardships. But no matter how dedicated to the cause one is, I knew very well that the loss of a body part is always traumatic, and that the more one talks about it, the better.

Manna said that for her it happened during fierce hand-to-hand combat. "The most shocking part comes when the anaesthesia wears off and you discover that your leg is gone forever." Manna's expression changed. "But that was a long time ago and it is not important. My situation was nothing compared to some of my comrades who had their limbs amputated without anaesthesia... it is not always available, you know."

"You don't really want to know about this stupid eye!" asserted Dehab, her wonderful smile lighting up her face and rendering the ugly socket even more grotesque. Then she suddenly changed the subject, exclaiming, "How lucky Ruth and Tamar are to have their mother here!"

The two women were clearly in the mood to talk about many other issues.

"Infibulation, circumcision..." began Manna, "you know, that damn practice handed down from mother to daughter? We hope it will be completely eradicated within a few years. It seems to be a thing of the past already in most of the liberated areas. To mutilate ourselves for the gratification of men! It is so sickening. I find it hard to believe that it seemed so natural when we were growing up — how cruel and dangerous it is when you think of it now.

"You know, Abeba, that many of the women who were mutilated this way when they were infants had complications during childbirth. Some even died, especially in areas where there was malnutrition or malaria."

"Speaking of the old traditions, I find dowries humiliating," Dehab cut in. "I'm glad we are finally seeing the end of that."

In that one-hour conversation, I could see that the lot of women was a burning issue in the lives of at least these two *tegadelti*; whether this was indicative of an entire trend I did not know. Later I learned that Manna had broken off her engagement to a military commander because of his chauvinistic attitudes. Manna and Dehab's concerns served as a signal to me that everything was not necessarily as it should be between the sexes in my homeland, just because women were taking part in combat and working alongside men. Women make up one third of the EPLF's army. Indeed it is incredible!

I was happy that these two *tegadelti* shared their concerns with me. When they asked if I would send them books on several different topics concerning women, I realized that they anticipated a tough time after independence.

On the evening of the third day, the head of the education

department, Beraki Gebreselassie, got married. Tamar told me that I had been invited but I did not want to go for fear of wearing myself out so early in my stay. She convinced me to go along, though, as it would be a short walk of only ten or fifteen minutes. Tamar beamed as she bathed Eskinder in a large pan with water from a bucket and dressed him in the new clothes I had brought him. Eskinder was so thrilled to have shoes that he could not take his eyes off them.

Beraki's wedding feast took place in two large rooms with fluorescent lights, doors, and mud benches and beds. As soon as we stepped inside the door, the aroma of the *zigni* hit me. Tamar told the two *tegadelti* who were acting as hostesses that I could not eat *zigni*, but I protested that I would have it just that once. My empty stomach coupled with the aromatic smell left me no choice. Eskinder was tired and wanted to go home, so I stuffed myself and went back to the hut without even talking to the bride and groom. I slept like a log and woke up feeling refreshed!

In the morning, I drank tea with my bread; and at lunch, instead of a handful of tasteless rice, I ate lentil *tsebhi* with *engera*. The chlorinated water suddenly tasted awful to me and I resorted to natural water, despite the advice of my doctor, and within a week totally got rid of my ailments.

All my body and my soul needed, was to be home.

In the afternoon I went to see Beraki in his office. The hut was graced with white painted burlap, its small window had curtains, the table with its comfortable chairs, and the shelves full of books made it look like a modern office in the middle of nowhere. Combat commanders and department heads of the EPLF do not only care about their subordinates work but also their personal well-being. Beraki shared with me how difficult it was in the beginning for Tamar to accept raising her son in Sahel. I was happy to hear that Tamar was a dedicated school nurse.

The fourth morning came, but still no sign of Ruth. I was really worried now. There were countless mothers, I knew , who had come home to Eritrea to see their sons or their daughters only to learn the hard truth that their children had been killed.

That evening, my aunt's husband, Yoseph, came to visit, as well as my cousin, Melashu, to whom Tamar had sent word. I had high hopes of seeing another favorite cousin of mine, Tedros.

Tamar was sure he was alive, but it was impossible to contact him on such short notice. He was in the front lines. The photographs of Ruth and Tedros that Petros had taken when he was in the field were reassuring, but I wanted to see him in the flesh.

Yoseph and I chatted almost the entire night. Much had happened since he had helped spirit the children and me out of Asmara on our way to the USA. Yoseph had been so heavily involved in the EPLF that he had no choice but to leave Meaza, and their small children behind in Asmara to join the struggle full-time.

They all decided that I should venture out to see the printing press and the famous five-mile-long hospital that had been dug into a cliff so as not to be visible from the air. Sertzu offered to stay behind with Eskinder. A car was made available, and at five in the afternoon we set out on our tour. We began with the printing press, but, unfortunately, an urgent meeting was being held there and no visitors were allowed.

Next came the hospital. First we tackled the dentistry department. It was dusk when we arrived and fluorescent lights were used to light both the outside and inside. I had heard much about the head of dentistry, Dr. Lainesh Ghebrehiwet, who is also Dr. Assefaw's wife, and on meeting her now, I was impressed with how professionaly she explained her work. My sister Lia was specializing in jaw, gum, and tooth reconstruction, and had studied under Dr. Lainesh. We spent some time watching the constant flow of *tegadelti* coming for dental work. There was a dentistry outpatient clinic as well as hospital facilities.

It was getting late, so we decided to spend the night in the hospital area. Tamar and I were given a tent that contained an army bed, and in the morning we had the opportunity for another mother-daughter chat. Again, I broached the subject of Tamar's eye injury, and this time she was more willing to talk about it.

"It was only my second round of combat," she began, growing very serious. "That day we had a long march. Our leader told us to duck behind the rocks while he checked the position of the enemy through his binoculars. I asked him if I could look through them. They must have caught sight of us, because we were showered with bullets. We were ordered to return fire. I started feeling dizzy and I saw blood streaming from my neck onto my chest. The fighting got more intense. 'Leave me here. Let me die. I'll only be a burden to you,' I said to my comrade who was trying to carry me on his back. He didn't listen but kept on carrying me and that is the last thing I remember." Tamar's voice was full of emotion.

"You were always a kind, caring child," I said. "And now I see the same Tamar — a mature woman, a loving mother, a true patriot. How do you stay this way? From everything I have heard, once a person is in combat, in the middle of all that gore, seeing your friends being killed, you get bitter and hard."

"Not with me, Mommy, nor with most of my comrades. I've shut out that combat experience. I can hardly even bear to think about it." The blood drained from her face. I could see in her eyes the pain of the memory of her fallen comrades.

"Let's just hope Eskinder and all the other Eritrean children will have a brighter future. Let's move on to another subject," I suggested.

"No, now that I've started I might as well tell you the whole story," Tamar murmured. "Two days later I found myself in our underground hospital. I didn't have much pain but I couldn't see a thing. It was a traumatic experience... but I made up my mind to live with it; my physical eyes may have gone, I told myself, but I still had my mental eyes, my mind. The shock and depression lasted only about three weeks. All the love and attention that I got from my fellow *tegadelti* helped me to cope." Now, try as I might, it was impossible for me to keep control, and I began to weep.

Three months later, Tamar continued, she was waiting for someone to take her outside when she saw the blurred image of people moving. Over the following months she slowly recovered. The optic nerve was permanently damaged, however, and she still could not see a complete face or read an entire line. She now has what is called "tunnel vision."

I thought of my mother and father at that moment, how wonderful it would be to take a Land Rover and drive to Asmara. They were only a day's drive from Sahel, yet they were so very far away, behind a barrier as impervious as the Berlin Wall. My brother Dawit was the only one who stayed in Asmara. He and his wife, Akberet, and their children lived with *Abboi* and *Addei*, I informed

Tamar, and by doing so, they brought some light into their lives. Dawit and Akberet had become the backbone of the tannery. I was sure, though, that Dawit felt very lonely, having been left behind by all his brothers and sisters. I had started corresponding with my parents a year after I left home, signing a false name, Letebrahan. *Abboi's* letters were encouraging most of the time, but I could read between the lines and knew it was all very hard on *Addei*.

Tamar and I stepped out of the tent.

The sun was shining on those majestic, bald mountains that looked as though they had been sculptured into the shapes of elephants and lions. The sky was a vivid blue dotted with snow-white puffs. Despite the sad story that had been the main subject of our sunrise chat, Tamar and I agreed that it was wonderful to be alive that morning. We walked around the area before the sun got too strong and at nine we joined the rest of our group for breakfast.

Saba Yohannes, who worked at the pharmacy — Ruth's sister-in-law — was our hostess, and we spent most of the day relaxing on the verandah of the pharmacy. There were desert flowers, and small pots of cactus on the well-swept stone floor. It was wonderful to have a long talk with Melashu, who had been wounded three times; she bore a large scar on her chin and another on her cheek.

Mengesha Amare, whom I had not seen for many years before he became a *tegadalai* joined us. Tamar had sent him a message upon my arrival. I was happy to see him. Mengesha told me incredible details about Mengistu's Sixth Offensive of 1981 — the infamous Operation Red Star. I asked two *tegadelti* in Port Sudan the whereabouts of my cousin Woldemichael Gebreab who joined the EPLF in 1977. I did not get a satisfactory reply. When I asked Mengesha if he had seen or heard from Woldemichael, I did not like the expression on his face when he answered "n...o." Then I decided not to press for more news for fear of hearing what I did not want to hear.

After lunch that day I could contain my worry over Ruth no longer.

"No paved roads, no telephone — but I know Ruth will be here," joked Yoseph.

I noticed Saba slipping out at one point and then returning with another woman, but I paid little attention since at the time I was deep in conversation with Yoseph and Mengesha.

"There is someone here," said Saba casually. I simply nodded in their direction and said *"Selam"* — Hello — and continued talking. But the guest kept on walking towards me, and as I glanced at her I noticed that she wore a special smile. I did a double-take and gasped, and then I jumped up and fell into Ruth's arms. Tamar rushed to join our embrace. The entire verandah was perfectly still.

After we dried our tears I took a good look at my other *tegadalit* daughter. Ruth still had that beautiful light brown skin and she looked perfectly healthy. But after I had observed her legs and felt her hands and shoulders I perceived a definite change: She had looked much stronger in the photograph she sent us a year earlier.

Melashu, Mengesha, and Yoseph, who had taken a three-day leave to see me, had to return to their duties, and Saba had to get back to work as well. A quiet moment followed. It was one of those times when a long-awaited dream has come true and you just cannot believe it.

The last day of January 1975 came to mind, when we had huddled together in the family room during the first battle in Asmara... and then the years before that, and those that followed.

Soon we were joined by Ruth's husband, Kidane Solomon. The last time I had seen Kidane was in early 1977 in Addis Ababa. Who would have dreamed then that one day he would be a son-in-law? I shared with him the snippets of news about his family that I had picked up through letters from his sister and mutual friends. Kidane's mother was a kind, gentle woman, and I knew how close he was to her, especially after the death of his father. He did not verbalize it, but I could tell how much he missed her. His respect and care for my Ruth was so obvious that my heart glowed.

At five o'clock a Toyota Land Cruiser came to take us back to the hut. We shared the ride with two *tegadelti* passengers. Our driver was a cheerful *tegadalai* who kept telling us about the various foreign visitors he had been meeting. At one point along the way, he stopped, climbed a cliff, and returned with a box. When I asked where he had gotten the parcel — we seemed to be in the middle of nowhere — he replied:

"The dentistry department."

Then he noticed the puzzled look on my face. "Haven't you been there yet?"

It was hard to believe. What I had seen by night — the large, sparkling rooms with windows and curtains, desert flowers and creeping plants, with a steady stream of human traffic — was now seemingly a hill just like any other

It was then that I was totally assured that no matter how many millions worth of arms it receives from any superpower or how many foreign mercenaries it gets, Ethiopa would never be able to get to our hospitals or our workshops; and it would never be able to liquidate our heroes, our *tegadelti*.

I had only a few days remaining and I wanted desperately to conserve my new-found energy, so I curtailed my tours. The grandmotherly instinct was slowly materializing, and Eskinder was also getting used to me.

Most of my time was spent in the hut with my daughters and their families, cousins, and old friends. We all talked quite a lot about the old days in Asmara as well as about life in the liberated area. My daughters, of course, wanted to know everything about our life in the United States.

Ruth, Tamar, and I cuddled up on the mud bed the first night all three of us were together. We did not close our eyes until well past two o'clock. They asked me all sorts of questions about their father, sisters, grandparents, and all their other relatives and friends. They wanted to know about the Eritreans in America — whether they were committed to the cause.

My daughters could not believe it when I said that their father, who had been king of the castle among seven women — wife, four daughters, and two maids — had adjusted so well in his shrunken household that even though he didn't cook he kept the kitchen meticulously clean.

Ruth and Tamar were very emotional on the subject of their sisters, although they did not express their feelings outright. They asked how Muzit and Senait talked, laughed, and dressed. They both said they wanted Muzit and Senait to get the best education possible — what they did not have or could not find they wanted for their sisters; but clearly they were both worried that Muzit and Senait would become too "Americanized."

They enjoyed it when I told them about the pillow fights that Muzit and Senait would have shortly after they arrived in the United States. They laughed at my story about how Muzit and Senait had believed the father of a friend who told them that their sisters had shot down an Ethiopian plane, and how they had come running home to our apartment in Virginia to tell us about it.

They found it difficult to grasp that Demekesh and Medhin, the aunts they had seen off to pursue their education in the U.S. years before, were now married, and they were happy to hear that Mengesteab and Haile, the husbands, were members of the Eritrean Students' Association in America; who would discuss women's issues and try to apply their belief in women's rights. The three of us agreed that this was quite a change from the traditional Eritrean relationship between the sexes.

But when Tamar asked about *Abboi*, Ruth stiffened up. I was puzzled. "Don't you want to know about your grandfather?" I asked. "It's just that I'm afraid of what I might hear," Ruth replied with emotion.

They knew that Solomon was married to Michealin, and they both asked if I had a photograph of the couple. I did have one that had been taken on their wedding day. "What a sweet smile Michealin has!" said Tamar. Her parents, Gabriela and Woldu, had been my gracious hosts in Khartoum. Ruth and Tamar had met Elsa, Petros' wife, in the field when they were still engaged, but they were anxious for me to bring them up to date since I had just visited them. We all marveled at how a new generation of the family was sprouting up in foreign lands.

"But hurry up and tell us about Michael!" urged Ruth. Michael was in the United States pursuing his education. There had been times in these past few days when I had to remind myself that these two mature women were actually my daughters. I secretly longed for the sweet teenagers I had known. But their faces lit up when we talked about Michael, and I was thrilled to catch a glimpse of my carefree, fun-loving children. Ruth and Tamar had been great childhood friends with Michael, Dawit, and Lia, and every one of them hungered for news of the other.

How I wished Lia, Tedros and Woldemichael could have

been with us when we were exchanging family news! It had become clear to me that the fighters missed their parents, their brothers and sisters, and all their loved ones despite the fact that they made great efforts not to appear sentimental. My daughters told me that they did their best to keep in touch with each other by letter in the field, and they managed to get together occasionally.

"What was your most unforgettable experience?" I asked Ruth hesitantly, wanting to share her worst moments yet at the same time reluctant to make her relive painful memories. She took a deep breath and looked at me as if trying to recollect. God has endowed my Ruth with a sharp mind and I know that she won the respect of her comrades in whatever capacity she served the cause — teacher, "barefoot doctor" or arms depot manager. At that moment I thought of how her father and I dreamt for her to study medicine or journalism. Although her first combat duty had been overwhelming, Ruth replied, it was the news of her sister's blindness that had most shaken her. When she heard about the injury three weeks after Tamar had been wounded, she walked for several hours to see her. Tamar was sitting outside the hospital entrance, her head shaved, with two tegadelti. "Tamar," Ruth called. "That sounds just like Ruth — who is it?" asked Tamar, looking in the direction of the voice. It was only then that Ruth was forced to believe what she had heard, that her younger sister was blind. *Tegadelti* were expected to conceal their emotions, but the shock proved too much for Ruth and she broke down and wept.

In the morning, Eskinder woke up crying, and Tamar got up to get him something to eat. He ate a few biscuits with tea, and then he dozed off: he was still terribly weak from the diarrhea.

After our breakfast of tea and unleavened bread, the three of us sat on the bed, Eskinder in my arms, and studied the photographs I had brought. Their father, Ruth and Tamar thought, had not changed since they had seen him last. But their sisters, in their tennis outfits and their hairdos, looked very different. Of course, twenty-year-old Muzit, and Senait, now sixteen, had been only twelve and eight when their sisters had tearfully boarded the truck that day in Keren.

"So many years have passed without us sharing their

lives," said Ruth wistfully. Tamar wondered, "What will it be like when we finally do meet again?" They looked at each other and then at me, and once more we all felt sad and got misty-eyed.

Although my two *tegadelti* lived a rough life in a rough environment, it had not hardened them to the joys of family love. I could see that they missed their sisters terribly.

They went back to the summer of 1972, when Ruth, Lia and Tamar travelled with *Abboi*, Mesfun, and I to Italy, Switzerland, England, and the United States. We all spent four days in Rome and a week in Switzerland. Then we went on to England where we left the three children for the whole summer at the Moral Re-Armament centre in Tirley-Garth. There they met youngsters their age of several nationalities as well as many interesting adults.

*Abboi*, Mesfun, and I returned home after a three-day stopover in Milan. Then, at the end of the summer, Mesfun flew back to London to pick up the girls and they all crossed the Atlantic to New York and Washington, returning home via Paris. The Coliseum, St. Peter's, Westminster Abbey, Buckingham Palace, the stately homes, the wonderful experiences with our friends in England, the Empire State Building, the Lincoln Memorial in Washington, the sidewalk cafés of Paris — was all still fresh in their minds.

The next day Tamar's team celebrated our reunion by slaughtering a goat and making *zigni*, a treat reserved for very special occasions. With freshly-baked *engera* and *sewa*, the atmosphere was festive and delightful. Word must have gone out, for *tegadelti*, especially women, came to visit us from all over the surrounding areas.

Eskinder's health seemed to be improving. He was eating a little better and was crying less, so Tamar began to relax. Together with Ruth she was busy the whole day welcoming and seeing off their comrades. They all wore versions of the same outfit — khaki, denim, or any other drab-coloured pants. Their only uniform was the plastic sandals that were manufactured in Sahel at the underground shoe factory.

The next evening, we attended a cultural show. The group had hastily constructed a makeshift stage and there was a program of folk dancing and singing from the nine "nationalities" of

Eritrea, as well as EPLF revolutionary songs. The show took place in the open air and at night, but the infinite inky blue sky filled with stars, the bright lights of the stage, and the music and dancing were like something out of *The Arabian Nights.*

During the intermission, they played European rock'n'roll tapes and the children raided the stage to dance to the music. Eskinder, who was just a year and a half, wanted to join in and a boy of about seven took him by the hand and brought him along to the stage. Eskinder's face was very bright under the lights; we could see him looking in our direction to make sure we were all watching as he jerked his tiny body in time with the pop music.

Four days before I left, a large meeting was held nearby and hundreds of *tegadelti* flocked to the area. This was a golden opportunity for me to see old friends. One of these was Alemseged Tesfai, whom Muzit, Senait, and I had seen eight years previously in Keren on our way out of Eritrea. The effects of time and the rough life in the field showed in Alemseged's face, but he was as humorous as ever.

The second person I had the chance to see was Semere, Kidane's brother, who had joined the EPLF from Sweden in 1972. I was happily surprised to see him after so many years. We had no more than five minutes together, but Semere said he had an important message for me. I expected it would be a note for his mother, but the next day I received a letter, and what follows is a rough translation from Tigrinya:

"My dear sister Abeba: You have no idea how happy I was to meet you after so many years. Just seeing you there brought back wonderful memories of our life in Asmara. Thanks to the enemy, we are where we are now, but regardless of how invincible the enemy appears to be, we will end up winners. The truth always prevails in the end. I want to say one thing to you, though. The suffering will stop much sooner if every Eritrean abroad talks about our plight. I know you and Mesfun were aware long before many: your involvement in welfare activities is proof of this. It may not be easy for you, but tell all your old friends, make new friends, get hold of the media — let the world know about us. We are humans too. We have the right to exist in peace. Besides, we have a case in the United Nations. You are a mother of two *tegadelti* and mothers will be sympathetic to you. See you in Asmara."

Semere's message was not for his mother, nor his sister, nor any other member of the family that he had had to leave behind. It was for all humanity.

Ruth and Tamar echoed Semere's sentiments: "Tell the world, Mommy. It is not for the love of guns that we are here; it is for the love of our country, and all humanity." It kept hitting me that these were not my teenagers, with their pony tails and mini-skirts, but seasoned *tegadelti*, women mature far beyond their years. The movements of the *tegadelti* are restricted to the mountains of Eritrea, but their minds are liberated. In those frail bodies lay enormous hearts and minds.

As I said goodbye to Ruth, Tamar, Eskinder, their families and friends, and the many *tegadelti* who came to see me off, my heart told me to remain behind with them. But as much as I wanted to stay, I felt like rushing to my Muzit and Senait as I never had before — to make up for everything that I realised I had missed in their lives.

The first two years of our life in the United States were very hard for me. Added to my homesickness were my painful separation from Ruth and Tamar, my having witnessed the death of a *tegadalai* in Khartoum, and my memory of the torture inflicted upon my fellow prisoners.

I was very careful not to give a clue to my daughters of the suffering I was going through. But regardless how hard I tried to hide it, Muzit and Senait noticed whenever I greatly felt the pain, crying my heart out. Would they be affected by all this? Senait still had one older sister to look up to, but both of Muzit's older sisters were far away, in a totally different world; and it was undeniable that I had been preoccupied all those years with the welfare of Ruth and Tamar, my family, and my country. I had tried to make true Eritreans of my daughters within a strong American culture. Was I really right in doing so?

It was Muzit's first tennis lesson and she wanted her parents to be there. We *were* there in body, but where was my heart? And what year was it? Why did I not take a photograph of her? Or did I?

And Senait's first high dive. Did I stay long enough to applaud her?

Did I express my happiness and appreciation when Muzit received a glowing report in junior high school? Did I tell her how proud I was when she became an honor student in high school?

When Senait saw how frightened I was after the first big snowfall in Washington she came running to hold my hand so that I would not slip. Was I as sensitive to Senait as she was to me? Why had we not taken them to Europe, when the opportunity had come up, or to some of the fascinating places in the United States?

Muzit was already in her second year of university, and Senait was in the tenth grade. Have I missed out on something in their lives? I wondered. But then I reminded myself that Muzit and Senait had both turned out to be loving, responsible girls; that they always talked about their sisters, their grandparents, their homeland.

And what about my husband? I gave Mesfun my all.

With all these ideas racing in my head, we arrived in Beref, where we would be staying overnight. We were in a valley between high cliffs that looked burned and desolate, and it was unbelievably hot.

As I climbed out of the Land Rover I wanted to wait for Lia and Tedros. I also had the urge to go back to Ruth and Tamar. But I tried to reason out that they are adults and all that I could do was to accept and respect the path they have chosen. Still, it was hard to forget Eskinder's little hand waving goodbye as the driver started the engine and the Land Rover moved further and further away from them; he kept on waving and waving until all I could see was a tiny speck in the distance.

I felt I was being torn into two. The pain was almost unendurable: I longed to be with the rest of my family in America. Yet half of me wanted desperately to stay; the agony of leaving was nearly too much for me to withstand.

But had Semere not written me a touching letter asking me to tell the world about the cause? Had not Ruth and Tamar and their many *tegadelti* friends expressed the same feelings? Had I not made a vow to myself to work on behalf of the countless numbers of Eritreans who had been stripped of their human rights? I remembered with fondness all my cellmates... Semhar, Fana, Ribka, Tsegga, Saba, Berekti, Genet, Hiwot, Sister Weini.... in our painful season.

Perhaps I could reach the world directly by way of the written word and convey Eritrea's stubborn hope.

And by four o'clock the next morning, as I boarded the Land Rover that would take us away from Eritrea, in the slightly cooled morning air and under cover of darkness, I had a distinct idea of what I would write.

My mind was clear and my soul was at peace.